GOLF SECRETS

GOLF SECRETS

JAMES A. FRANK

All inquiries should be addressed to: Burford Books, Inc., PO Box 388, Short Hills, NJ 07078.

Printed in Canada.

10 9 8 7 6 5 4 3 2 1

Library of Congress Cataloging-in-Publication Data
Frank, James A.
Golf secrets
James A. Frank.
p. cm.
ISBN 1-58080-011-4 (pbk.)
1. Golf. I. Title.

GV965.F725 2004
796.352—dc22

2003019094

CONTENTS

4. FAULTS

5. SHOTMAKING

6. TROUBLE PLAY

7. SHORT GAME

8. PUTTING

9. SAND PLAY

10. STRATEGY

11. ...AND MORE

ACKNOWLEDGMENTS

Thanks go to many people, starting with Jerry Langdon, sports managing editor for the Gannett News Service in Washington, D.C. Jerry came to me in the late 1989 with the idea of a golf column. He explained that they wouldn't pay much money and they couldn't force the newspapers subscribing to the service to take the column. How could I refuse?

I'm indebted to my good friend Chris Carey, who introduced me to publisher Peter Burford, and who spent countless lunches talking about books—this one and others.

The photographs were taken by Fred Vuich, *Golf* Magazine's staff photographer and a frequent travel/golf companion. The model is Chris McVeigh, former assistant golf professional at Rockland Country Club in Sparkill, New York. Thanks also to the former head pro at Rockland CC, Keith Larsen, who generously let us use the course, the driving range, and Chris's time.

Thanks to everyone at *Golf* Magazine: You're certain to see bits of your work in mine.

To Willy and Rebecca, who very kindly went to bed early, which gave me quiet time to write—one column a week, 25 weeks a year, for four years.

And to Belle.

INTRODUCTION

I've often wondered how the early golfers learned to play.

Who taught the shepherds of Scotland, standing around with nothing to do but watch a flock of dumb sheep, to swing their crooks at rocks?

Who taught Mary Queen of Scots—who was beheaded a few days after being seen playing on the links rather than mourning her murdered husband—about weight shift and reaching a parallel position at the top (no mean feat in a long dress, high collar, and crown)?

Who taught those haughty British gentlemen of 200-plus years ago, whose portraits hang today in clubhouses from John O'Groats to Land's End?

Sorry, but I'm not going to fill in the history of golf instruction. Honestly, I don't really know, other than that most golfers learned from watching others. Of course, there was always someone to give advice.

As long as there have been caddies, they've offered an opinion—requested or not—on their players' inability to hit the ball straight. The first golf professionals, who made more of their living making and selling clubs and balls than they did playing, were very influential, role models for the glut of new golfers who teed it up once mass-produced equipment made the game cheaper, starting about the mid-19th century.

My point is that golf grew quite nicely, thank you, without much in the way of institutionalized instruction. Before golf books—the first instruction volume was published in the United States around 1890—before magazines, before golf schools, long before videos and computerized swing analyzers, golf soldiered on.

Today, with so much instruction available, the game has never been more complicated.

When golf arrived in the United States at the end of the 19th century, there was only the St. Andrews swing. But now you can choose from different swings being taught by numerous teaching pros. Arms straight, wrists bent, legs apart, head up, butt out—and somebody else swearing "no, no, no, it's just the opposite." It's enough to make a person go back to tennis. (Okay, not that bad.)

When Jerry Langdon, managing editor of the Gannett News Service, asked me to write a column of golf instruction years ago, he said he wasn't looking for more complexity. He wanted simple ideas and quick tips that any golfer, regardless of skill level, could understand.

Great. I hadn't mastered the St. Andrews swing, let alone "Connection," or pronation, or square-to-square. I'd be damned if I was going to foist it on anyone else.

What I did want to offer was help—immediate and uncomplicated—shots anyone could pull off the next time they played. Read it in the morning, use it that afternoon.

A few more yards on the drive. Fewer three-putts. Cures for the faults that plague us all—the slice, snap hook, top, thin, chili-dip, and worst of all, the "S" word (that's shank, but I didn't say it).

The columns that follow were written to give a little help real quick. Say, five minutes each. They cover the field: address, tee shots, common faults, the short game and putting, shotmaking, trouble play, even a little strategy.

Find your problem. Read. Give it a try. Don't worry who taught Queen Mary. I hear she never kept her wrists firm: something about ruffled sleeves.

—Jim Frank

GOLF SECRETS

ADDRESS

All About Alignment

Get the Right Address

Get a Good Grip

Perfect Posture

Where's the Ball?

ALL ABOUT ALIGNMENT

No matter how well you do everything else in a golf swing—choose the right club, take your grip, control your tempo—the shot won't go where you want if you aren't properly aligned. In fact, most bad shots are caused by incorrectly aiming either the club or the body.

A common misconception is that the body points directly at the target. (The target can be the flag, a spot in the fairway, wherever you want the ball to land.) But because you stand to the side of the ball, your body should be parallel to the imaginary line running from the ball to your target.

To align yourself correctly, imagine you're standing on a railroad track: The ball is on the outside rail, which points to the target; your feet are on the inside rail. The rest of your body also is aimed down the inside rail. This is called setting up "square."

If your body points at the target, you are in a "closed" position, actually aiming to the right. (Reverse the directions for lefties.) From this stance, you'll probably hit the ball to the left. Similarly, if you're "open" to the target, aiming left, you'll likely hit to the right.

It's easy to slip out of square, so regularly check your alignment. Place two clubs on the ground, one by the ball pointing at a target, the other across your toes. The two clubs should be parallel.

Another way to ensure a square setup is with a preshot routine. Before every shot, stand a few feet behind the ball and envision the target line. Walk to the side of the ball and plant your right foot. Keeping a light grip, place the clubhead behind the ball, pointing down the target line. Bring your left foot into position, readjust your right foot, then firm up your grip and you're ready to swing.

To help you align the clubface, aim it at intermediate target. When you're behind the ball visualizing the target line, pick out a spot—an old divot or leaf will do—on the line a few feet in front of the ball. Aim the clubface at this spot as you settle in at address.

A perfectly square stance. The feet, knees, hips, and shoulders are parallel to the target line.

In an open stance, a right-handed golfer aims his body to the left of the target. This tends to produce a slice.

In a closed stance, a right-handed golfer aims his body to the right of the target. This tends to produce a hook.

A proper stance. Note the slight bend at the knees and hips (not the waist). The arms hang loosely from the shoulders.

Feet are shoulder width apart. Weight is distributed evenly between the heel and ball of each foot.

GET THE RIGHT ADDRESS

Just like mailing a letter, your ball won't find its intended location if you don't start with the right address. Here's how to avoid some of the most common address mistakes.

STANCE

Your feet should be about shoulder-width apart. If your stance is too narrow, it won't support your weight at the top of the swing, resulting in the body swaying. However, if your stance is too wide, your hips will lock, inhibiting a proper body turn.

Take a proper shoulder-width stance while facing a full-length mirror. Then measure the distance between your feet with the club that lets you align one foot with the bottom of the shaft, the other at the end of the grip. Refer to that club when you need to reestablish your stance during practice and on the course.

POSTURE

The body should flex at two main points: the hips and knees.

Many golfers bend at the waist rather than the hips, which restricts body turn. But even if you do bend at the hips, it's possible to go too far, which forces the shoulders to turn unnaturally and leads to a steep swing and a slice. Check the clubhead for a telltale sign of "stooping": If the toe is off the ground at address, you've bent over too far.

Flex the knees enough to feel your body weight on the balls of the feet. Not enough knee flex often leads to the above-mentioned stooping, whereas too much flex makes the upper body straight and stiff.

ARMS

Many golfers stretch their arms away from the body in an effort to reach the ball. Although extending the arms may feel powerful, it actually cuts power by creating upper-body tension. Instead of making a swing, you chop at the ball, usually resulting in a slice.

Set your arms last, after taking your stance and flexing the hips and knees. Let the arms hang loosely from the shoulders, the right elbow bending naturally. There should be a six- to eight-inch gap between your thighs and hands.

GET A GOOD GRIP

It's one of golf's unarguable truths: If you don't have a good grip on the club, you won't make good shots. The hands are your only contact with the club, so how they hold it is vital to making a successful swing.

There are three types of grip. Whichever you use, keep the hands parallel to each other at all times or they won't perform as a single, coordinated unit.

OVERLAP

Also called the Vardon grip after turn-of-the-century British golfer Harry Vardon, who popularized it, this is the grip of choice, especially among top players. The little finger of the right hand overlaps the left hand, falling into the channel between the left index and middle fingers.

INTERLOCK

The right little finger intertwines with the left index finger, linking the hands. This grip is often recommended for players with small hands.

10-FINGER

This grip resembles the hold on a baseball bat, with all 10 fingers on the grip and the right little finger butting up against the left index. Many new golfers start with this grip, then change as their game improves; but that doesn't mean the 10-finger style can't work for you.

The three grips:
1) Overlap

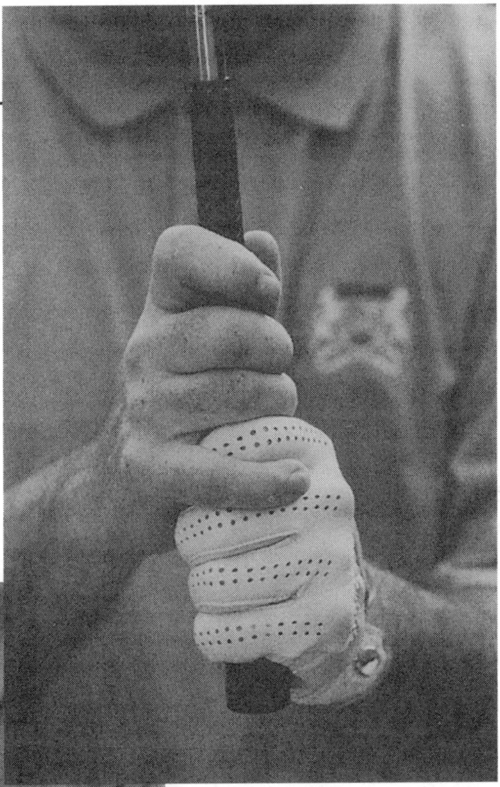

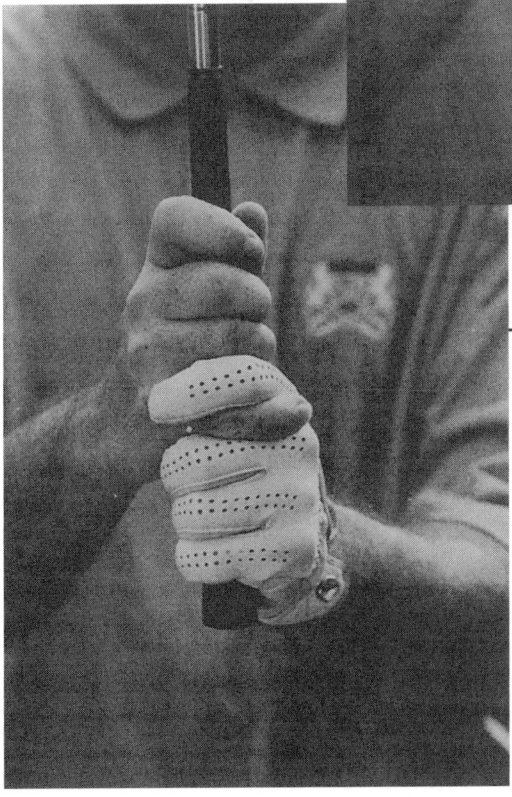

2) Interlock

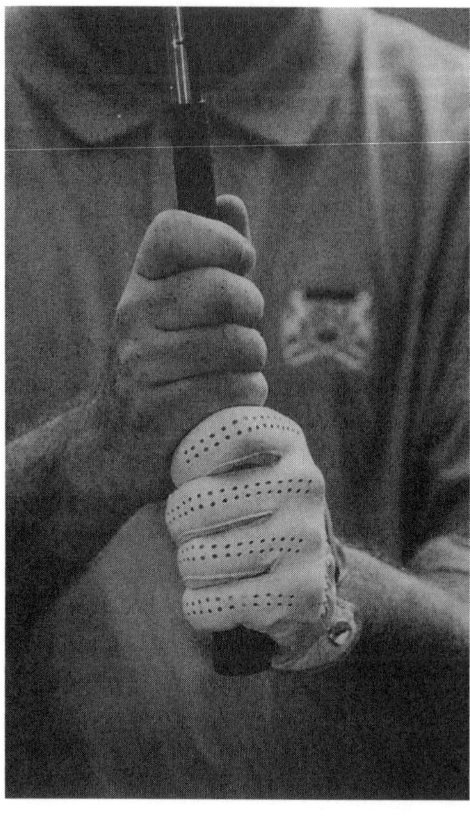

3) 10-finger

GRIP PRESSURE

How tightly or loosely you hold the club has a bearing on your shots. A grip that's too tight can block the proper release of the hands so the clubface is open at impact, sending the ball to the right.

A loose grip can result in the club flopping around during the swing—which leads to all sorts of problems—as well as too much closing of the clubface so the ball curves left.

Your grip should be tight enough that the club can't move around in your hands during the swing, yet light enough that you can make an unrestricted waggle at address.

One of golf's enduring clichés is that you should think of squeezing an open tube of toothpaste as you take your grip: Hold the tube securely, but don't squeeze so hard that any toothpaste would squirt out.

PERFECT POSTURE

Do your shots fly high and to the right? You might be standing too tall at address, which causes a steep swing. Or is a low, right-to-left shot more your style? Maybe you're too bent over and swinging around your body.

How you stand at address influences how the ball flies. If you're too straight or stooped over, stretching out your arms or stiff in the knees, your swing—and the shot—will be affected. Here's how to perfect your posture for solid shotmaking.

SIMPLE SETUP

Without a club, stand up straight. Flex your knees as if starting to sit down. Bend slightly at the waist, but keep your back straight and your head up; dropping your head on your chest pushes the upper body forward.

Flexed and relaxed, let your arms hang down naturally and bring your hands together. They should be six to eight inches ahead of your thighs. You are now standing properly. Grab a club and repeat the procedure.

COMMON PROBLEMS

Many players, especially new golfers and high-handicappers, extend their arms out trying to "reach" for the ball. This position creates tension and a chopping swing that leads to a slice. Be sure your arms are hanging loosely from the shoulders, not straining to reach away from the body.

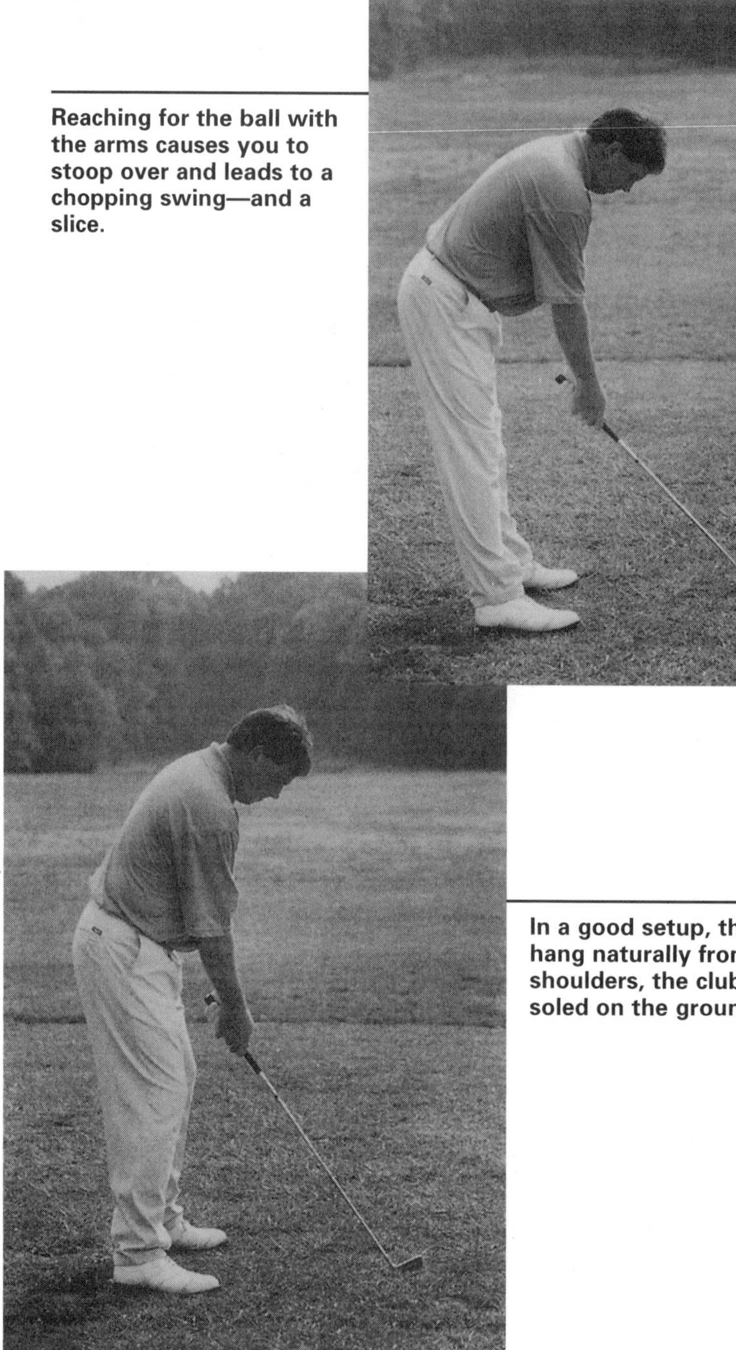

Reaching for the ball with the arms causes you to stoop over and leads to a chopping swing—and a slice.

In a good setup, the arms hang naturally from the shoulders, the clubhead soled on the ground.

Check your knees. Straightening the legs is a common fault that produces tension and restricts lower-body action, which leads to all sorts of bad shots. After getting in position, flex your knees once or twice to keep them loose and springy.

A PROPER FIT?

The final test, of course, is with a club. If you assume a proper posture but the club isn't soled (that is, the bottom of the club isn't flat on the ground), you may need to have the lie angle of your clubs adjusted. If the toe end of the club is off the ground, your shots will tend to fly left; if the heel is up, the ball flies right.

If you can't comfortably sole your clubs, ask a qualified clubfitter—a club pro or perhaps someone in an off-course golf store—for help fitting your clubs to your swing.

WHERE'S THE BALL?

Ball position—the placement of the ball between your feet at address—should depend on your skill level.

Pros and other good players, who have a consistent swing, prefer to position the ball in the same spot every time, usually on line with the left (front) armpit. That spot approximates the lowest point of the swing arc, which means the clubface will be in its optimum position at impact, as well as the same time after time.

To locate your low point, take a few 5-iron practice swings without a ball; where the divots begin indicates the bottom of your swing.

If you're like most amateurs, however, your swing is neither perfect nor consistently repeatable. Therefore, you'll probably benefit by changing ball position, especially when hitting mid- and short irons. With these clubs, move the ball back in your stance an inch or two. This will help you make a more descending swing, so the club hits the ball before meeting the ground. Shots will get up in the air with the maximum amount of backspin.

As you move the ball back, be sure to move your hands slightly forward. Besides ensuring the proper descending blow, this helps create a smooth, accelerating swing by encouraging the hands to pull the club into the ball on the downswing.

SPECIAL SHOTS

No matter where you position the ball for normal shots from the fairway, there are some situations that demand moving it to the front, middle, or back of your stance. Here are a few of the more common ones.

Depending on the lie and shot you want to play, position the ball back...

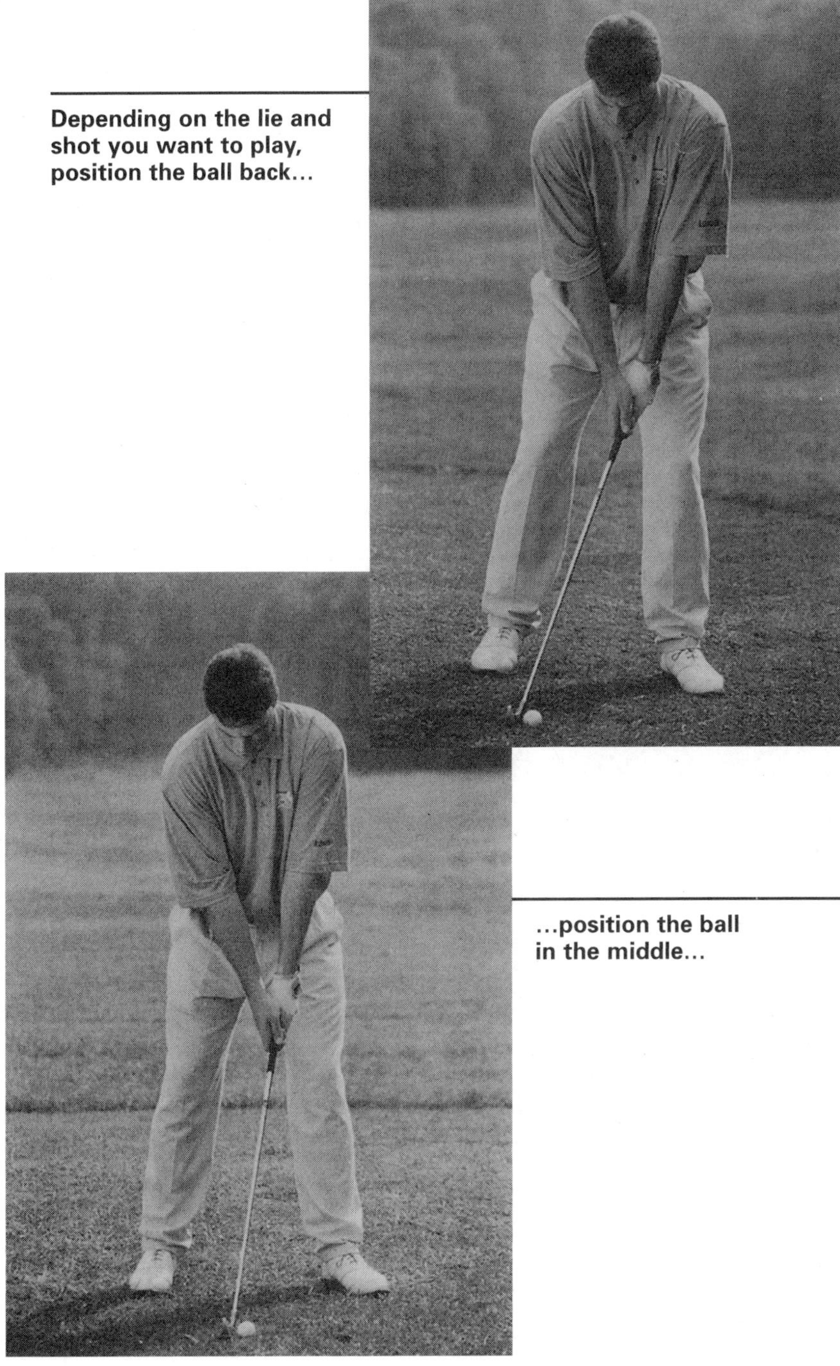

...position the ball in the middle...

...or position the ball forward in your stance depending on the lie and shot you want to play.

Ball Back (sets up a sharply descending blow)
From a downhill lie, against back lip of bunker, in divot hole.

Ball in Middle (slightly descending blow)
For a chip shot, pitch-and-run, buried lie in bunker, punch (and other low shots under branches or wind), shot from rough that runs after landing.

Ball Forward (impact made on upswing)
For the basic drive, basic bunker shot, against front lip of bunker, uphill lie, lob (and other high shots meant to stop after landing), putt.

OFF THE TEE

Conquer the First Tee

Power Tips

Tactics on the Tee

Power Plays

Put Away the Driver

CONQUER THE FIRST TEE

Jack Nicklaus says his most important shot is the first drive of the day. For Nicklaus, and most of the rest of us, the first shot sets the tone for the entire round: Hit a good one and you're brimming with confidence; hit it poorly and you're beaten before getting started.

Here are some tips to help you hit a good first shot, and keep the good feeling throughout the round.

MAKE THE MOST OF THE PRACTICE TEE

One way to put extra pressure on your opening tee shot is to make it your very first shot of the day. Hit at least a few balls on the practice range. Don't overdo it: At least loosen your muscles and get a feel for your swing. Hit enough practice balls that the clubs don't feel strange in your hands.

VISUALIZE

Before hitting any shot, you should see it in your mind's eye—setup, swing, and successful result. This is especially important on the opening shot when you need to calm the butterflies and block out the many distractions around the first tee. So before standing over the ball, think about what you want to do and "see" it happening.

PICK A TARGET

Wanting to put the ball somewhere in the fairway isn't enough. Pick a target—a spot, a sprinkler head, an imaginary flagstick—to focus your attention.

Tee up your ball so something—a leaf, spot, or other recognizable spot—lies directly on the line between your ball and final target.

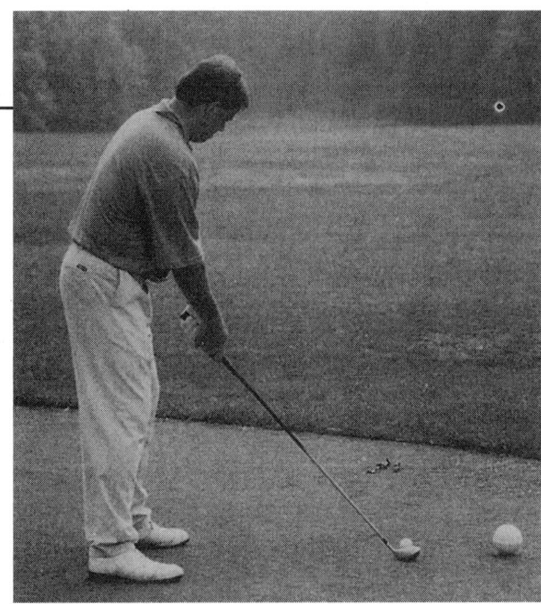

PICK THE RIGHT CLUB

If the driver hasn't been treating you well lately, don't expect it to perform on the toughest shot of the day. Use a club you have confidence in, be it a 3-wood, 3-iron, whatever. Forget about distance and play for accuracy.

SWING FOR LESS

Rather than trying to kill your opening drive, think about hitting it shorter than usual. Planning for less distance will promote a slower, more compact swing—and probably drive the ball farther than what you're used to. If it works, swing for less on all your tee shots.

RELAX

Take a deep breath, then exhale deeply. Shrug your shoulders, shake out your arms and legs, get loose—then swing.

POWER TIPS

Looking for a few extra yards? Who isn't? Try these shortcuts to longer shots.

IT'S IN THE FINGERS

Check that the grip hasn't slipped in your hands from the fingers to the palms. This fault blocks the natural hinging of the wrists, and allows the clubhead to twist at impact.

The grip of the club should lay diagonally across the fingers of the left hand, from the tip of the index finger to the base of the pinkie.

In the right hand, the club should lay across the base of the fingers, just above the palm. Then wrap the palm and thumb over the top of the club and the left thumb.

LENGTHEN THE CLUB

The longer the club, the longer the shots. You can add to the effective length of the shaft by taking hold at the very end of the grip, so the butt presses into the heel of your left hand. Practice to get the feel for swinging a "longer" club.

SETUP CLOSED

Aiming slightly to the right of the target has two power advantages: 1) It promotes hitting a right-to-left draw, which runs a few extra yards after landing; and 2) It gives your shoulders and hips a head start to making a big turn.

Holding on at the very end of the grip lengthens the club for longer shots.

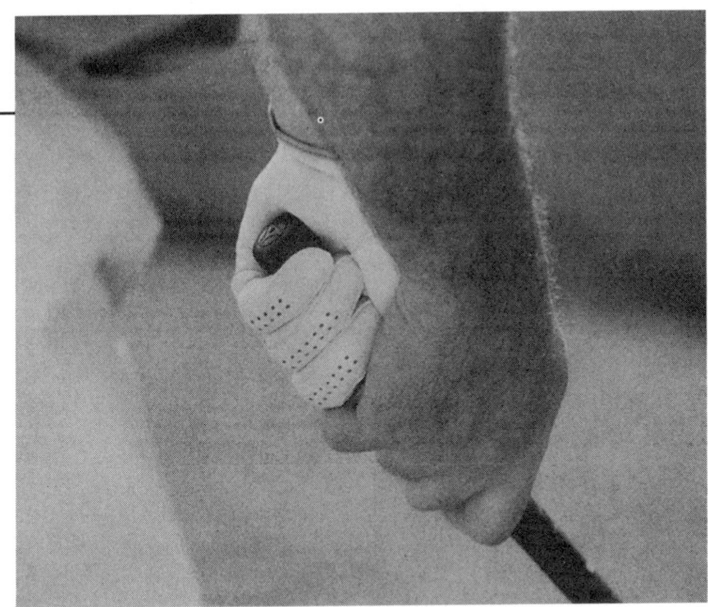

Hover the club off the ground to encourage a long, low, one-piece takeaway—and to produce a big backswing.

If you have a hard time closing your body at address, take your normal setup, then pull your right foot back from the target line about two inches. Let your body shift into position with the feet before swinging away.

HOVER THE CLUB

Address your tee shots with the clubhead raised slightly off the ground, the sweetspot directly behind the ball. Hovering encourages a long, low, one-piece takeaway and eliminates the possibility of snagging the clubhead in the grass going back.

RAISE THE LEFT HEEL

Standing flat-footed during the swing limits your turn. If your legs are far enough apart to create a stable foundation, then try lifting the left heel as you near the top of the backswing. (If you sway or fall over, your base isn't solid.) But don't lift the foot straight up—roll it so the left instep remains on the ground.

After pausing at the top, start the downswing by replanting the left heel. This move provides another power kick, ensuring that the lower body leads the upper body into impact.

TACTICS ON THE TEE

At least 18 times a round, you're allowed to hit from a perfect lie—the tee. Although you can place the ball wherever and however you like, many golfers don't take full advantage of their options.

The "teeing ground," according to the Rules of Golf, is not only the line between the two markers, but a rectangle two club lengths deep. That means you can move back as far as seven feet (about the length of two drivers). Although you'll probably stand all the way up on par-fours and fives, this depth helps when you're between clubs on a par-three: Stepping back a few feet can give you confidence to make a full swing rather than trying to hit it "easy" from the front line.

Furthermore, only the ball must be inside this area; you may position your feet outside it.

Teeing the ball well to the right or left within the box lets you play a hole wisely. For example, when trouble is on the left side, tee the ball far to the left and aim back to the right. This enlarges your safe landing zone.

Move around in the box to find a level lie. Starting with the ball above your feet will cause it to curve to the left (for right-handers); a ball below your feet turns right. Of course, shaping your shot this way can help if the hole bends or if you're aiming to a particular side of a fairway or green.

Teeing up or downhill also affects ball flight. From an uphill lie the ball goes higher and shorter; from a downhill stance the shot flies lower and longer. You can create the same results by varying tee height. Start with the ball teed up for a high shot, which you might want for riding a tailwind. Tee it down for a low shot, which will bore into a wind blowing at you.

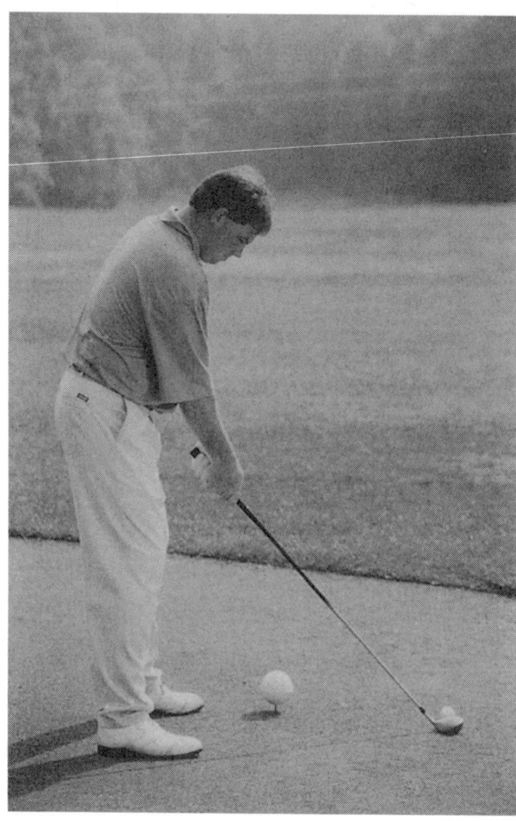

You don't have to stand within the tee markers if your ball starts there. Teeing up well to the side can help you play a hole more strategically.

Finally, don't expect tee markers to point you the right way. Some architects deliberately angle tees toward trouble, or perhaps the greenskeeper was sloppy replacing the markers after mowing. Only trust what you can see: After putting your ball on the peg, step behind it and look to your target to determine the perfect line.

POWER PLAYS

Every golfer wants to hit his or her tee shots longer, but in trying for more power, many players tense up or swing too fast, which creates wild, short drives. Try these mental and physical tips to add yards to your shots.

Walking to the tee, stay loose and relaxed, and keep your mind free of too many thoughts. If you tend to tense up over the ball, lighten your grip, which will relax your arms and allow you to start the club back smoothly, or think about keeping the legs flexed and springy, important for making a good weight shift.

Another positive thought is to strive for a big follow-through. Trying to finish with your arms high and the club behind your back makes you

Take the club back long and low for a longer backswing—and longer shots.

Try to finish the swing with arms high and the club well behind your back.

less conscious of the ball, which will allow you to concentrate on making a good swing.

The right frame of mind will help you hit the ball longer, but only if your body is up to it. Two physical keys that will benefit everybody's driving are to widen your arc and stay behind the ball.

Widening the arc means swinging the clubhead as far as possible away from your body, so it travels a longer distance and has more time to build up speed. To widen your arc, keep your wrists firm as you draw the club away from the ball. Breaking the wrists too early brings the club to the top too quickly, cutting the swing short. Extend the clubhead straight away from the ball as long as you can; it will rise naturally as the shoulders turn.

Staying behind the ball is nothing more than starting the downswing with the legs. Many golfers mistakenly begin the downswing with their arms, which means the upper body gets ahead of the lower body and the legs never contribute.

Once you've reached the top of the backswing, kick off the downswing by sliding your knees toward the target. The arms then can drive the club through the ball with the benefit of the legs' power.

PUT AWAY THE DRIVER

Simply because the first shot on most holes is called a "drive" doesn't mean you must use a driver. In fact, sometimes the driver is the worst club to hit.

If you're wild off the tee, a driver will add to your problems. Its long shaft (43–45 inches is standard) and low-lofted clubhead (8 to 12 degrees) make the driver hard to control while producing the sidespin that creates slices and hooks.

Most golfers carry 3- and 5-woods, which work off the tee as well as from the fairway. Other equipment options include the 2-wood, which has about 13 degrees loft, and the 1-iron, a club that most amateurs avoid: The secret to the 1-iron is letting the club do the work rather than trying to "lift" the ball into the air.

Even if the driver doesn't give you trouble, there are times when a fairway wood or long iron is your smart choice off the tee. Here's when you should think twice about your designated driver.

SHORT DOGLEGS

You don't want to run the ball through the fairway, which will leave a second shot from rough—or worse.

HAZARDS TO CARRY

Sometimes course architects dare you to try flying a water hazard or fairway bunker. Don't fall into their trap. Lay up short of trouble if only a perfect drive will carry it.

PIN POSITION

If the hole is cut on the left side of the green, the smart approach probably is from the right side of the fairway, but staying to the right might demand laying up off the tee.

TAILWIND

When the breezes blow with you, a 3-wood makes sense because it launches the ball high where the wind can take it.

TIGHT HOLE

Faced with a pressure drive through a chute of trees, take a club that you're sure you can hit straight. There's a huge psychological benefit to be gained by hitting your next shot from the fairway, not the woods.

Play the course, not some macho game that demands bashing the ball off every tee. If you think of the drive not just as a long shot but as the key to setting up the rest of the hole, your scores will improve.

THE SWING

Pull the Trigger

What a Good Swing Feels Like

The First 18 Inches

Tame Your Tension

Sweep the Fairway Woods

Tempo and Balance Work Together

Lash Your Long Irons

PULL THE TRIGGER

What's the most important moment of the swing? The pause at the top? Impact? No. For most amateurs, the key moment is the first one, that split second of transition between standing motionless over the ball and moving the club.

How the swing begins influences everything that follows. If you start with a jerk, the ensuing motion will never be smooth. If you start from a standstill, your muscles will remain tense. To make a rhythmic, relaxed swing, you need to kick it off with a "trigger."

Besides moving the muscles—so the swing begins from a fluid, rather than static, position—a trigger can help correct your faults. One of the following triggers should help your swing start right.

FORWARD PRESS

One of the most common triggers involves sliding the hands an inch or two toward the target as a prelude to turning the shoulders. Be sure to keep the left wrist firm: Breaking the wrists (often the result of sliding the hands too far) shrinks the size of your swing arc, robbing you of power.

SWIVEL THE HEAD

Jack Nicklaus starts every swing by turning his chin away from the target. Besides eliminating upper-body tension, this clears the chin out of the way of the left shoulder, promoting a bigger turn.

There are two common "triggers" for beginning a smooth backswing. The first is turning the chin away from the target.

KICK THE RIGHT KNEE IN

If you sway during the swing or finish with your weight on the back foot, try pushing the right knee toward the target as your trigger. This action fights the reverse weight shift by getting your body weight moving to the left side from the get-go.

OPEN THE HIPS

If your lower body refuses to contribute to the swing, resulting in a loss of power, start by twisting your hips slightly open (to the left of the target). Besides eliminating lower-body tension, this move helps clear the hips so the arms whip through impact.

The second common trigger is kicking the right knee in toward the ball.

WAGGLE

The mini-swing that many golfers make before the real thing also can be an effective trigger. Besides putting the muscles in motion, the waggle can set particular shots. For example, if you want to try bending the ball from right to left, waggle the club a little more inside the target line to promote an inside takeaway; conversely, a left-to-right shot can be set up by waggling out-to-in. Then try to duplicate the waggle as you begin your actual swing.

No matter how you trigger or waggle, don't freeze your body before beginning the swing. Pull the trigger, then fire!

WHAT A GOOD SWING FEELS LIKE

One reason many golfers can't make a good swing is they don't know how it should feel. The following will help you appreciate a good swing by describing the proper sequence of actions and the movement of your weight—a key to what we "feel"—from address to follow-through.

ADDRESS

Balance your weight between your feet as well as between the ball and heel of each foot. Be sure to flex your knees or the weight will stay back on your heels.

BACKSWING

Don't think too much about what initiates the swing. When you are relaxed and in balance, simply swing your arms freely so the club moves away from the ball. If your upper body is relaxed, the arms will pull the shoulders, which turn the hips and the left knee. Your left foot should roll inward, indicating that your weight is shifting from the left side to the right.

AT THE TOP

Whether or not you actually pause at the top of the swing, you want to think you do. At this point, the backswing ends and the downswing can begin; if you don't pause, the two overlap and you're heading for trouble. Your weight should be loaded up on the inside of the right foot.

DOWNSWING

If you've made a pause, the downswing can begin correctly—with movement of the lower body. Whether you initiate the downswing by twisting your hips, shifting your weight back to the left foot (planting the left foot on the ground is a good trigger), or sliding your legs toward the ball, be sure the upper body hangs back until the lower body is in the lead.

Once the legs move and the hips begin to unwind, the upper body starts uncoiling in reaction to the lower body's actions. As the shoulders unwind, they'll pull the arms down toward the ball. Don't throw the arms at the ball or turn the shoulders prematurely: Let them follow the lower body.

IMPACT

The key here is balance. The last of your weight is flowing from the right side to the left: The left foot is flat on the ground and the right is coming up, turning onto its big toe. As the club swings through, your weight follows.

FINISH

Although almost all your weight is on the left foot, you should be in balance and relaxed. A good test is to hold the finish position—weight forward, hands and club high—until the ball lands. If you can do that, chances are you made a good swing.

THE FIRST 18 INCHES

How you swing the club over the first 18 inches—the takeaway—can lead to disaster. Your initial move away from the ball sets up the shape of your swing as well as its tempo and the angle of attack. So concentrate on the start of the swing to ensure success at impact.

LOW TO THE GROUND

Don't lift the clubhead to start the swing. That means you're cocking the hands and wrists instead of the turning the shoulders. A wristy takeaway inhibits proper body action and shrinks your swing arc. As a result, shots are weak and offline.

Keep the clubhead low, dragging it along the ground as long as possible. Your hands and wrists should be firm, but not locked, as your shoulders turn. If you're doing it right the clubhead will brush the top of the grass for about 18 inches before rising naturally. Don't help the club up.

Groove a low takeaway by practicing with a tee placed on the target line 18 inches behind the ball. Turn the shoulders and keep your arms extended, sweeping the clubhead back until it hits the tee.

TO THE INSIDE

Some teachers suggest dragging the clubhead straight back along the target line. That can work, but also may produce big slices if you don't reroute the club to the inside on the downswing.

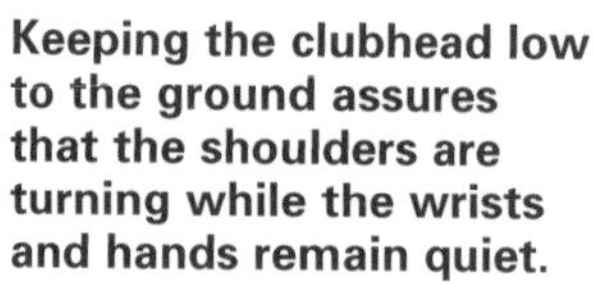

Keeping the clubhead low to the ground assures that the shoulders are turning while the wrists and hands remain quiet.

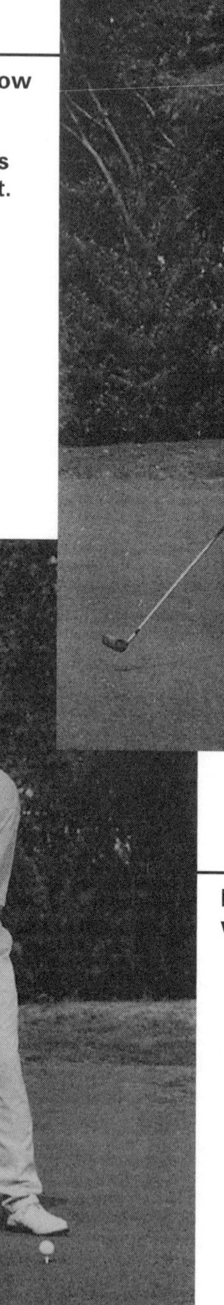

Practice a low takeaway with the "tee drill."

At about the time the clubhead starts to rise, it also should move to the inside. Don't resist this rotation. Allow the turning of the upper body to bring the club to the inside naturally.

SMOOTH

The takeaway should be a smooth, one-piece motion. Don't worry too much about speed; proceed at your normal tempo. But you must be fluid, sliding the club back from the ball without any sudden movements that could ruin your timing and feel.

If you're having trouble making a smooth start, try hovering the clubhead. Hold it about an inch off the ground at address, and keep it raised as you begin the takeaway. Hovering promotes a big shoulder turn and keeps the clubhead from snagging in the grass behind the ball.

TAME YOUR TENSION

You want to drive that little white ball a long way, so what do you do? Grit your teeth, take a firm hold on the club, tense those muscles, and take a big, hard swing.

What happens? If you're lucky enough to hit the ball at all, it probably slices lazily off to the right and into the woods, a lake, or some other on-course oblivion.

What went wrong? Tension. Standing over a stationary ball, it's easy to tighten up, which makes the ensuing swing short and stiff—and unsuccessful. Here are the parts of the body most susceptible to tension, with some ways to relax them.

GRIP

If your grip is too tight, that tension will spread up through your wrists and arms and into the upper body, killing any hope of making a free and easy swing. Squeezing the grip too hard also inhibits the arms from releasing through impact, a major cause of inaccuracy.

So how tight is right? Enough to maintain a sure grip, yet light enough that the club could be pulled from your hands by someone tugging the head. Many instructors suggest pretending you are clutching a small bird: Squeeze firmly enough that it can't fly away, but don't crush it.

UPPER BODY

Even with a relaxed grip, it's possible to be as tight as a drum around the chest and shoulders. Before picking up the club, let your arms hang

Grip the club just tightly enough to hold on, but not so hard that someone tugging at the other end couldn't pull it out of your hands.

free and shake them to loosen the muscles. Shrug your shoulders to relax the neck, chest, and upper arms, and shake away the tension that inhibits a full, free turn.

LEGS

If your legs are stiff or straight, it's virtually impossible to drive them toward the target in the downswing, which means you won't generate any power from the lower body.

The best way to loosen the legs is by bending the knees. Flex your knees, bouncing up and down to reduce the tightness in your legs. Maintain that knee flex in the swing from address to the follow-through. You'll be rewarded with newfound power and accuracy.

SWEEP THE FAIRWAY WOODS

One of the most versatile tools in the golfer's bag is the fairway wood. It can knock the ball a long way from the short grass, light rough, even most fairway bunkers.

Yet these clubs give many amateurs fits. Why? Because they're not sure how to swing them: Do you want to make contact on the upswing, like a driver, or with a more downward blow, like along iron? The answer: Neither.

Fairway woods should make contact at the bottom of the swing, as the clubhead "sweeps" across the turf. Here are the fundamentals of the sweep swing.

STANCE

Spread your feet shoulder width apart. Divide your weight evenly between the feet.

Bend at the hips, but not too far. Too much bend promotes a steep, descending swing and effectively shortens the shaft, which will shorten your distance. Stand far enough from the ball that your arms have an unimpeded path through the downswing.

Start with your hands in line with the ball so the clubhead sits flat on the ground. Pushing the hands forward, which lifts the back of the head, creates a descending swing.

BALL POSITION

The ball shouldn't be quite as far forward as for the driver, but not too far back, either. Off the left heel is usually about right; you may want to

Feet shoulder width apart, ball forward in your stance (off the forward heel), and hands in line with the ball.

experiment. Remember, the farther back you play the ball, the steeper the swing becomes.

SWING

If you want the club to come into the ball moving parallel to the ground, then that's how you should take it back. Make a low takeaway, brushing the clubhead against the turf as long as possible.

Probably the most common mistake is making an arms-only swing rather than a full-body turn. An arms-only motion leads to an up-and-down "chop" swing and a high, weak slice.

On the downswing, imagine the club traveling parallel to the ground as it nears, then meets, the ball. Strive for a full finish to ensure hitting through the ball.

FROM SAND

Hitting a fairway wood from a bunker requires a few changes in technique. Spread your feet an additional two inches apart and move the ball back to the middle of your stance. Play this shot only if the ball sits cleanly on top of the sand and if the lip of the bunker is low.

TEMPO AND BALANCE WORK TOGETHER

Tempo and balance, crucial to the success of every shot, go hand in hand: You can't stay in balance if your tempo is off, and you won't have good tempo without balance. Here's how to find and keep them.

TEMPO

This is the speed of the swing, from address to finish. Every player has a perfect tempo: Tiger Woods and Nick Price swing naturally fast, Ernie Els is slower. They've found their best swing speeds, which often match their pace of play, temperament, and so on. If they tried to change, their swings wouldn't be nearly as effective.

Your optimum tempo is the speed that lets you stay in balance, control the club, and generate good clubhead speed. Maybe you want to think about swinging at 80 percent, as Sam Snead suggested, or count "one-two" as you swing, taking the club back on "one," starting the downswing on "two."

Whatever image you choose, practice it to ingrain your tempo. Learn what feels too slow and too fast. Watch your shots to see how they react.

BALANCE

To make your best swings, your body weight must be properly positioned throughout the swing. That's balance.

At address, balance your weight between your feet. Spreading the feet too far apart or bringing them too close together will throw off your balance. So will leaning too far to either side. Center your body

You'll know you've made a good swing when you finish in control, with most of your weight on the outside of the front foot.

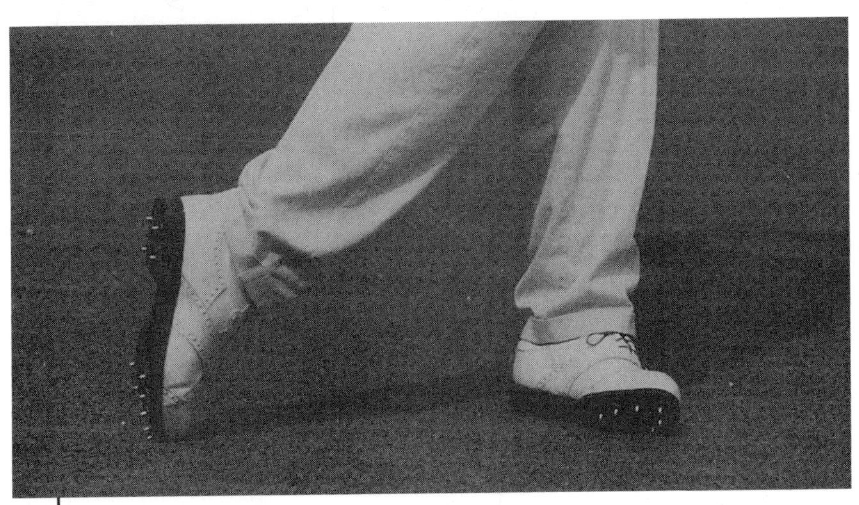

And the back foot turned up on its toe.

above the ball. Try to feel comfortable and loose, and ready to spring into action.

Good balance lets you swing at your tempo. Your weight must flow easily to the back foot on the backswing, then to the front foot on the downswing. Anything other than a smooth weight transition means problems with tempo, balance, or both.

The best test of balance is at the finish. When the swing is done, nearly all your weight should be on the outside of your front foot, while your back foot is turned up and resting on the toe. If you can reach that position and hold it comfortably for three seconds as you watch the shot, you're doing just fine.

To learn both balance and tempo, take practice swings with your feet together. Hit a few balls that way in every practice session and you can't help but groove your right speed and improve your balance.

LASH YOUR LONG IRONS

What is it about long irons that make them so terrifying? Stand over a 2- or 3-iron and you'll see. That little head and flat face seem to scream out, "Here comes a slice!" or a "top" or a "smothered hook."

Long irons have a bum rap. Even the dreaded 1-iron has more loft than the average 3-wood, so hitting it high and straight should be easier. Long irons are perfect for teeing off on short par-fours and hitting into tight greens, if you can get over the fear.

Mastering long irons begins by altering your setup and takeaway. Make these adjustments to expand your shotmaking.

SETUP

To understand how you address a long iron, consider how you want to finish. At impact, the clubhead should be sweeping the ball off the grass, shaving a thin divot. Compare that to the steep swing of a short iron, which digs into the ground and dislodges a big piece of turf.

To sweep, start with the ball forward in your stance, off your front instep or heel (experiment to find your optimal position). At address, your hands should be in line with, or just slightly ahead of, the ball; pushing them too far ahead encourages a descending blow. Also begin with your head behind the ball.

TAKEAWAY

The first 18 inches away from the ball are crucial. The takeaway must remain low to the ground, so don't break your wrists. Make a one-piece takeaway, turning the shoulders and arms together away from the ball.

A sweeping swing begins at address with the ball forward in your stance and hands in line with or just slightly ahead of the ball.

This builds a big arc and keeps the wrists quiet.

Your impact position should mirror the setup: head and upper body behind the ball, hands in line, the club sweeping through. Don't try to help the ball up—that leads to a topped shot. Instead, make a smooth swing and trust the club to hit the ball high, long, and straight.

OFF THE TEE

On a long par-three or short par-four, use a long iron and make the same swing described above. Tee the ball so it sits about half an inch off the ground. You want to sweep through impact, catching the ball slightly on the upswing; teeing the ball low promotes a descending blow.

If you're still having problems, play the ball even farther forward in your stance, at least on line with your front instep. Then sweep it clean!

FAULTS

Learn from Your Ball Flight

Straighten Your Slice

Two Common Mistakes:
Thin and Fat

Bad Advice

The Ugliest Shot in Golf

LEARN FROM YOUR BALL FLIGHT

Whether you've been playing golf for years or have just begun, you have the ability to be your own teacher. By watching how your shots fly, you can determine—and begin fixing—your faults.

Ball flight is determined by two variables: the path of the club on the downswing and the position of the clubface at impact. Study your shots to deduce the variables that created them, then make corrections.

SWING PATH

In a perfect swing, the club approaches the ball from inside the target line, is square to the target at impact, then comes back inside in the follow-through.

A common fault is the inside-out swing, approaching the ball from inside, then pushing the club to the outside (toward right field). Most shots off this swing start to the right; where they finish is determined by the clubface.

If the face is square to the inside-out path, the ball sails dead right, called a push. If the face is closed (aiming left), the result is a roundhouse hook, starting right then curving left. With an open face (pointing right), the ball bends right to right.

To counter an inside-out swing, bring the club straight back as long as possible in the takeaway.

An outside-in path brings the club into the ball from the far side, then moves it toward left field. Shots from this swing begin left. If the clubface is square, the ball flies dead left, called a pull. An open face makes the ball curve sharply left to right. A closed face makes the ball curve even further left.

In a good swing, the club approaches the ball from the inside and is square on the line at impact.

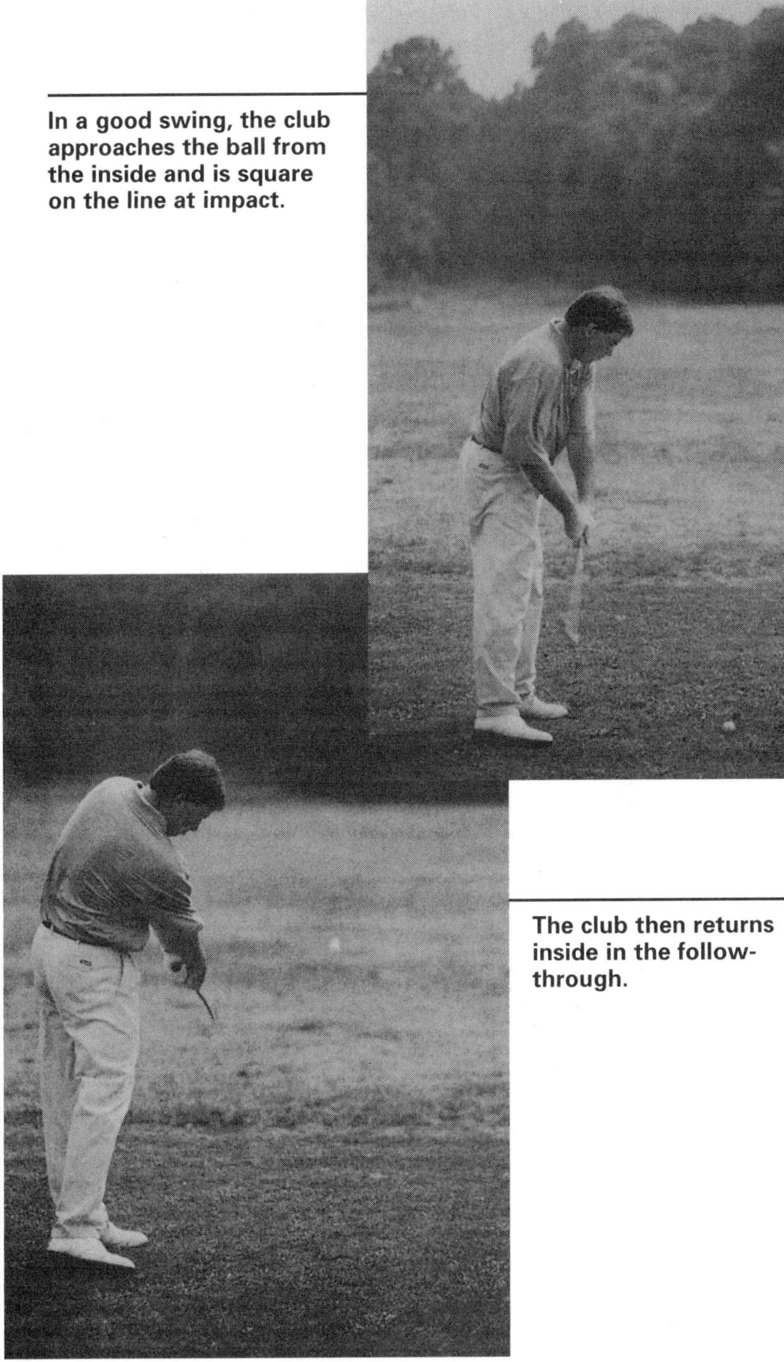

The club then returns inside in the follow-through.

Correct an outside-in swing by bringing the club inside the line in the takeaway.

A proper inside-square-inside swing starts the ball straight. Any subsequent movement is the result of clubface alignment: Off an open face, the ball bends right; a closed face curves it left.

CLUBFACE ALIGNMENT

Ideally, the clubface is square at impact, aiming in the direction of the swing path. If you've determined from watching your shots that the face is open, strengthen your grip at address by turning the hands slightly away from the target. If the clubface is closed, weaken your grip by turning your hands toward the target.

STRAIGHTEN YOUR SLICE

The banana ball is one of the ugliest shots in golf and one of the most common. If it's your shot, these tips will help you go straight.

SET UP SQUARE

At address, your shoulders, hips, knees, and feet must be parallel to the target line (the imaginary line from the ball to your target). During practice, place a club across your toes and the other key spots to check for proper alignment.

STRENGTHEN THE GRIP

Most players who slice have weak hands or a weak grip. In either case, the hands don't roll over at impact, so the clubface is open (pointing right) when it meets the ball. Encourage a proper "release" of the hands by strengthening your grip: Turn your hands away from the target so that at address the "V"s formed by the thumb and forefinger of each hand point toward your right shoulder.

DON'T CHOKE THE CLUB

Hold it tightly enough so you're in control, but loosely enough that someone could tug it out of your hands.

HANDS AHEAD

Many slicers start with the hands behind the ball. At address the left hand should be ahead of the ball so a straight line could run down the left arm, through the hands, to the ball.

Two ways to turn your slice into a straight ball: Begin with a strong grip.

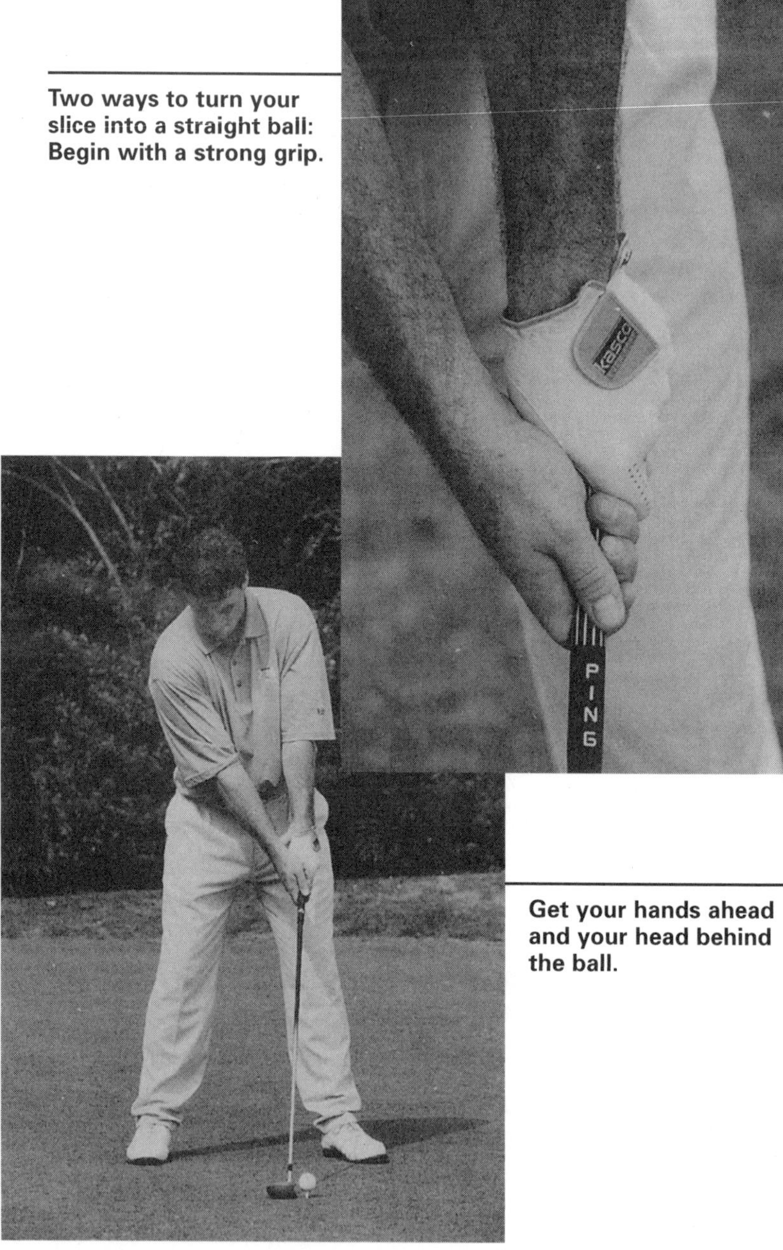

Get your hands ahead and your head behind the ball.

HEAD BEHIND

If your head isn't behind the ball at address, chances are you aren't shifting your weight properly in the backswing. Encourage the head-back position by swiveling your chin to the right—as Jack Nicklaus does—before starting the swing.

ONE-PIECE TAKEAWAY

Starting the club away from the ball in "one piece" means moving the body parts together. Visualize your arms as two long sides of a triangle, with the base a line across your shoulders. When you start the backswing, think of turning the entire triangle—shoulders, arms, and hands, right down to the club—together. Furthermore, don't break the wrists too early in the backswing: Let them hinge naturally as the club swings up past waist height.

SOLID RIGHT SIDE

Body sway during the swing leads to poor contact. Keep the lower body still by using your right leg as a brace. Don't stiffen it so much that you can't make a good turn, but keep it firm so it can support the swing.

TWO COMMON MISTAKES: THIN AND FAT

Although every golfer is unique, the mistakes that plague them are not. Two of the most common are "thin" and "fat" shots. Thin means hitting the top of the ball with the bottom of the club. Fat is hitting the ground behind the ball. Here are the causes and cures.

HITTING IT THIN

After the slice, the thin or "topped" shot might be golf's most common fault. Rather than clubface meeting the ball flush, the club's bottom edge strikes the top half of the ball, sending it scooting along the ground. This shot produces inconsistent distance, whereas the low trajectory brings extra trouble into play.

The thin shot often results from trying to help the ball into the air. Many golfers don't trust a club's loft and downward blow to launch the ball skyward. Only a proper swing—a descending blow with the irons, a low sweep with the woods—gets the ball airborne.

Another common cause of the top is starting with the head too low or the body bent over. You may think starting in a crouch will help you stay down at impact, but the body straightens up during the swing, lifting the club.

The key is proper posture: Don't stoop or drop your chin on your chest at address.

HITTING IT FAT

The "fat" shot—sometimes called a "fluff" or "sclaff"—also has a variety of causes. If you're hitting fat with the irons, you may be playing the ball

Crouching over and carrying your hands too low leads to hitting it thin.

The fat shot results from playing the ball too far forward and breaking the wrists too early in the backswing.

too far forward in your stance. Move the ball an inch or two behind the front heel for iron shots.

If changing ball position isn't enough, you're either picking up the club too quickly in the takeaway or making a poor weight shift. In either case, keep your hands and wrists firm as the backswing begins, and turn, rather than tilt, your upper body.

Your weight should move to the back foot on the backswing, then to the forward foot on the downswing. If it's doing the opposite—a "reverse pivot"—your body will be moving away from (rather than toward) the target on the downswing and the club will hit the ground well behind the ball, sending it very high and very short.

BAD ADVICE

Some of the worst mistakes in golf come as a result of misinterpreting a piece of advice and turning it around until it hurts, rather than helps, your game.

Two of the most common—and destructive—examples of this are the phrases "keep your head down" and "keep your arm straight." Every golfer has heard them, but if you take these instructions literally, you'll never make a good swing. Here's what those directions really mean, and how to put them into practice.

KEEP THE HEAD RAISED

After hitting a bad shot, someone says, "You lifted your head." So for the next shot, you drop your chin until it's almost resting on your chest and the shot is no better. What's wrong?

Pushing your head down creates tension in the upper body and impedes a full shoulder turn back and through. Think about it: It's hard to turn your shoulders when your chin is in the way.

There's another problem. If your turning shoulder encounters your chin on the backswing, something's got to give. Either the shoulder stops turning, killing your turn, or the upper body sways away from the ball to get the chin out of harm's way. In either case, you won't produce a good swing.

So rather than lowering your head, lift it high enough to allow the shoulders to rotate under your chin. Then lower your eyes so they're looking down over your cheekbones at the ball.

Keep your head up—so your shoulder can turn under the chin—and your left arm firm, not straight.

KEEP THE LEFT ARM COMFORTABLE

No matter what anyone says, it's impossible to keep the left arm straight during a golf swing. You can try, but in doing so you'll tighten your left side, limiting your chance of making either a big backswing or a full finish.

Instead of trying to keep the left arm straight, let it feel firm, but not locked. It must be loose enough to extend as far as possible in the backswing. (Don't overdo it, bending the elbow so much that you severely shorten the length of your swing arc.)

As you bring the club down from the top, the force of the swing will straighten the arm so it is straight as it approaches impact. This is crucial if you want to hit long, accurate shots.

THE UGLIEST SHOT IN GOLF

The ugliest shot in golf is the shank, or as the British politely refer to it, the "socket." This horror occurs when the ball is struck by the hosel—that part of an iron that connects the head to the shaft—rather than by the clubface. The ball flies low, short, and sharply to the right, almost perpendicular to the target line.

There are many possible sources of the socket, from your setup to your swing. These adjustments will help you shake the shanks.

AT YOUR FEET

If you set up with too much weight toward your toes, you're likely to fall forward during the downswing. This shifts the swing plane forward as well so you hit the ball off the hosel.

Start with your weight distributed evenly between the heels and balls of your feet and keep it there throughout the swing.

IN YOUR HEAD

If your head drops forward during the swing, it means the upper body wants to take over and lunge toward the ball. This also shifts the swing plane forward, producing the shank.

To stop lunging, try to keep your head from moving down toward the ball. Don't tense up, which will restrict your swing, but think about holding your head in place.

A common cause of the shank is standing with weight toward your toes. This causes you to fall forward, toward the ball during the downswing.

IN YOUR HANDS

At impact, the hands and wrists should lead the clubhead into the ball. But if the wrists break early, the clubhead flips toward the ball, causing a shank.

Address the ball with the hands and wrists slightly ahead of the ball, then keep the wrists firm during the swing and impact. Don't make them so stiff they can't cock naturally on the backswing and coming down, but firm enough to maintain control.

Shanking is especially common off short irons, when you place the ball back in your stance. If so, position the ball forward, off the left heel. This gives the club extra time to square up before impact. Also try rotating the arms toward the target coming down, further encouraging a square clubface.

SHOTMAKING

Curve Balls

Sure Shooting

Learn to Throw the Punch

Four Soft Shots

Get It There!

Driver from the Deck

Know the Knockdown

Spin It Back!

CURVE BALLS

Most amateurs would kill to hit the ball straight, but there are times when you'll want it to curve. The ability to hit a fade, which bends left to right (for right-handed players), or a draw, which moves right to left, allows you to slide around trees, hit to a flag set on the side of the green, and steer away from trouble off the tee.

RIGHT-TO-LEFT DRAW

To bend the ball in either direction, start with two targets in mind: 1) where you want the ball to finish; and 2) the furthest point of the curve.

Set the clubface directly at your final target, then align your body toward the outermost spot of the curve. For a draw, that means aiming your feet, hips, and shoulders to the right of your ultimate goal. How far right you aim depends on the size of the obstacle: The further right you aim, the sharper the curve.

Swing the club on the path set by the body: That means swinging to the right of your final target. Avoid the temptation to steer the club back toward the target. Let the position of the clubface draw the ball back to the left.

LEFT-TO-RIGHT FADE

The fade is the reverse of the draw. Aim the clubface at your final target and aim your body to the left. How far left determines the severity of the curve.

The draw shot will run after hitting the ground, whereas the fade will sit down faster. That means a draw travels farther than a fade: You'll

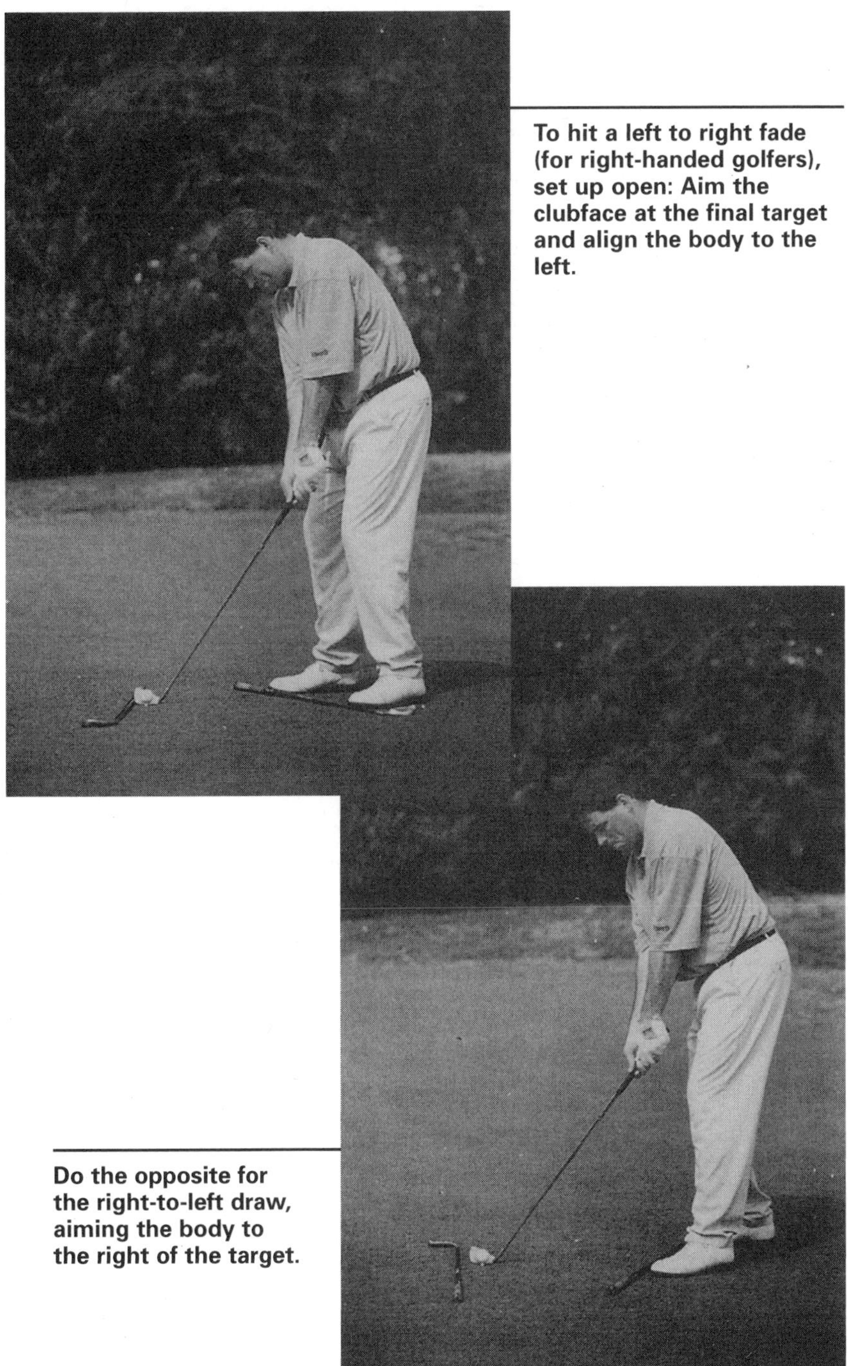

To hit a left to right fade (for right-handed golfers), set up open: Aim the clubface at the final target and align the body to the left.

Do the opposite for the right-to-left draw, aiming the body to the right of the target.

likely need one less club (a 7-iron instead of a 6, for example) when hitting a draw, and one more club for the fade.

Also, if you play cavity-back or investment-cast clubs, those advertised as more "forgiving" of bad shots, you might have a hard time making the ball bend. The same features that straighten out your bad shots want to straighten your curves, even when hit deliberately. Practice to see just how forgiving your clubs are.

Finally, the more the loft on the club, the easier to make the ball move. So if you find it simple to draw a 7-iron, the 3-iron might prove harder. That also means the intentional curve with the driver demands lots of practice.

SURE SHOOTING

Many golfers think accuracy means hitting the ball straight. In fact, an "accurate" shot is one that finds the target you picked. Here's how to make your shots hit their spots.

PLAN AHEAD

Accuracy begins in your head: Analyze and visualize. Don't wait to check out the situation until you're standing over the ball; begin analyzing—looking for unusual lies, obstacles, and your ultimate target—as you approach the ball.

Once you know what you want to do, visualize the shot in your mind, from a smooth swing to the ball landing. A positive mental image leads to a good swing.

ON THE TEE

Start with proper fundamentals, especially a relaxed, neutral grip and square alignment. Plan to play your normal shot—straight, fade, or draw. Position your clubhead first, aiming it at an interim target located a few feet ahead of the ball on your intended line of flight.

No matter what the situation, swing smoothly. If you're a little wild, shorten your backswing so it stops before parallel, then make a free downswing. Don't steer the ball; that's a sure way to spray. Also hold the club about an inch down the grip for added control.

Concentrate on a wide-open hole just as on a tight hole. Run through your normal preshot routine and aim for a particular spot, not simply "somewhere in the fairway."

Don't be macho: If you have more control with a 3-wood than a driver, give up a few yards for a better chance of finding the fairway.

FROM THE FAIRWAY/ON PAR-THREES

Know your normal yardage with each club. Then, when making a selection, don't expect to hit a "career shot" but your average-length poke.

When shooting for a green, weigh the pros and cons of going for the flag versus finding the safe center. Some pros won't aim at the hole with any club longer than a 7-iron; make your own set of rules, then stick with them unless you're in a match situation when only a heroic shot will do.

Finally, always plan ahead, set up square, and swing smooth.

LEARN TO THROW THE PUNCH

One of the most useful shots in golf is the punch, which flies low and straight and stops quickly after landing. It's the perfect shot when you're hitting into the wind, trying to keep the ball under overhanging limbs, or firing at a well-protected target.

You can punch with almost any club, but it's easiest with a medium to short iron, roughly 5-iron to wedge. When selecting a club, figure that you'll need one or two clubs more than for your normal shot; for example, if you hit a 7-iron 150 yards, use a 5- or 6-iron for a 150-yard punch.

Play the ball just behind the middle of your stance, which delofts the club for a lower trajectory and encourages hitting ball before ground for backspin. Swing easy, primarily with the arms keeping the lower body quiet. Make a three-quarter swing—the hands coming back no higher than your ears. Smooth, even tempo is important; decelerating on the downswing will cost in accuracy.

Keep your wrists firm and hands quiet on the downswing. The follow-through is short, with the club finishing about waist high: If it comes up any higher, you've swung too hard.

After mastering the basic punch, you can adjust the stance and swing to hit fades and draws. To hit the low fade, set up in an open stance with the ball off the left heel. Swing the club up to the outside, away from your body, then down to the inside. Remember to make a smooth, three-quarter motion. Shift your weight forward on the downswing and keep your wrists firm so the club is open at impact.

"Punch" it by playing the ball from the middle of your stance, making only a half- to three-quarter-length backswing.

To keep the ball low, finish low. Don't let your hands get above your shoulders.

For a low draw, set up closed, the ball in the middle of your stance. Swing to the inside going back, then to the outside coming down so your head feels as if it's staying behind the ball. Let the wrists release naturally.

The faded punch will stop very quickly after landing, whereas the draw will run. Take that into consideration when picking the club.

FOUR SOFT SHOTS

There is great satisfaction in hitting a ball hard, and golf offers plenty of opportunities for power: the big drive, digging the ball out of rough, shoveling out of sand, and more.

But golf is also a finesse game, and sometimes a slow, easy swing is necessary. Here are four situations where you should try hard to hit it soft.

THE CONTROLLED DRIVE

If you're having trouble taming an errant driver, try this soft swing, which will produce a safe, low-flying shot.

Choke down about an inch, play the ball off your left foot, and make a slow, shortened (about three-quarter length) backswing, keeping your left heel on the ground. Coming down, don't let your hands turn over through impact. You'll give up some distance, but you'll be able to find the ball. Use this technique when hitting into a wind and the drive must stay low.

HALF A 5-IRON

The average golfer hits a 5-iron 150 to 180 yards. But when you're under trees or battling wind, a shot of about half that distance might be your ticket home.

Play the ball a little behind the center of your stance and choke down almost to the metal of the club. Pick it up quickly (the right hand is in control), then make a soft but firm downswing and a shortened follow-through. Start with the clubface slightly open if you want the ball to check up; close the face for a shot that rolls.

Hit the soft, controlled drive by positioning the ball well forward in your stance and taking the club back only as far as the three-quarter position.

LOB FROM LUSH GRASS

From deep rough when you want the ball to fly high and stop quickly, use a sand wedge. Open your stance and the clubface, make a long, slow backswing (break the wrists quickly to get the club up), then swing down slow and steady. Pretend you're hitting an explosion from sand and slide the club into the grass about an inch behind the ball. Be sure to follow through so you don't decelerate coming down.

SHAVE FROM SAND

When your ball is sitting up in a greenside bunker, don't explode it out and take lots of sand, but shave it off the surface. Open your stance and the face of your sand wedge, swing back smooth and easy, and take a thin slice of sand starting about an inch behind the ball. It will fly softly, then roll a little way on the green.

GET IT THERE!

Next time you're watching the pros on television or in person, notice where their approach shots and putts end up. More often than not, the pro will get the ball to or past the hole (unless that would leave a tricky putt). It's one of the pros' commandments: Thou shalt not leave the ball short.

Amateurs should think the same way. To be sure of getting the ball to the hole, follow these three rules: 1) Don't get cute; 2) Take enough club; 3) Take a big enough swing.

DON'T GET CUTE

Whether you're trying to tack on a few extra yards with a deliberate draw or hoping to loft the ball in the air from a downhill lie, don't expect to hit a shot you don't own. Play the percentages and hit the smart, safe shot. Leave the experimentation for the driving range; once you've mastered a shot in practice you can bring it to the course.

TAKE ENOUGH CLUB

Know how far you hit each club and don't expect to suddenly gain 5 or 10 yards in the middle of the round. "Leaning on a 7-iron" probably will result in a bad shot when a smooth 6-iron would have done the job. Also, when you play with a long hitter, don't fall into the trap of trying to match his club selection. Use the club that's right for you.

TAKE A BIG ENOUGH SWING

"Never up, never in" is as true when you're hitting from the fairway as it is when you're putting: You have to hit the ball hard enough to give it a chance.

Ben Crenshaw says that there are four ways to miss a putt—left, right, short, and long. The only one you can easily rule out is short: If you stroke the ball hard enough, one of your potential misses is eliminated.

It's the same around the green. Many golfers leave short shots short. To cure that, try to hit every pitch, chip, and sand shot so it finishes 10 feet past the hole. You'll be amazed how often you'll hit it stiff.

DRIVER FROM THE DECK

It's rare to see an amateur golfer take the driver out of his or her bag anywhere other than the tee. But many pros hit the big stick from the fairway or light rough when the conditions are favorable. It's a gutsy shot that average players can master.

Hitting the driver off the deck makes sense when you need distance, the landing area is wide, you want to keep the ball low (e.g., under the wind), or you need a miracle to get back into a match. But you can't crash a driver unless the lie is right.

To ensure flush contact, the ball must be sitting up in the grass or light rough. Test the conditions by hovering the clubhead behind the ball; without pushing it into the grass, check to see if any part of the ball is higher than the face. If it is, you can play the shot. If the top of the ball is in line with the top of the club, the shot is risky. If the clubface is higher than the ball, forget it!

The swing resembles that of a normal drive, with minor changes. You must make a long, low takeaway and a sweeping swing, so widen your stance about an inch—keeping the ball positioned off your left (front foot) instep—and shade your weight to your right (back) foot. Bend a little at the knees, and hold this extra flex throughout the swing. Finally, choke down half an inch or so on the club; this shortens your swing for control.

Make a smooth, slow backswing. On the downswing, resist the urge to lunge at the ball. Feel as if you're staying behind the ball through impact. Then keep the club low in the follow-through.

The conditions—and your stance—must be perfect. Make sure the ball is sitting up in the grass. Then play the ball forward and make a long, low, sweeping swing.

Some clubs handle this shot better than others. Most metalwoods carry extra weight toward the sole, making it easy to get shots airborne. Many metalwoods also have rounded soles, which glide through the grass. Finally, the shallower the clubface, the easier the shot: Many of the new "oversized" drivers simply can't make this play.

KNOW THE KNOCKDOWN

Whether you are an experienced golfer or a new player, there is one specialty shot you should have in your bag—the knockdown.

The knockdown is a low-flying shot made with a shortened swing. Because the swing is restricted and the trajectory low, the knockdown offers accuracy, which is important when playing into the wind, hitting to a well-guarded green, and escaping from under tree limbs and other overhanging obstacles. The knockdown also can help you stay straight in a crosswind; it's less likely to be blown off course from the side.

WHICH CLUBS?

The knockdown is an iron shot, from 4- or 5-iron to wedge. You can't take anything longer because you must make a descending blow, and longer clubs need a more sweeping swing.

Practice to determine how much distance you lose with a knockdown. It might produce the same distance as your normal swing, but chances are you'll lose about one club's yardage, which means hitting a knockdown 6-iron when you'd ordinarily play a full-swing 7. Also experiment to see how quickly the ball stops after landing.

Club selection is especially important from under trees, where you must consider both trajectory and distance. If you need a less-lofted club to stay under the limbs, you may have to shorten your swing even more to reduce distance.

HOW TO HIT IT

Play the ball back in your stance, an inch or two behind center. Choke down on the club and move your hands ahead of the ball. Start with

Get the ball back in your stance, choke down, and angle your hands ahead to set up a descending downswing.

most of your weight on the left side. All of the above encourage a descending blow.

Your wrists must remain firm throughout the shot. Don't swing back farther than three-quarter length, hands shoulder high. For the downswing, pull the club down hard with the arms and upper body, keeping the lower body quiet.

The shot won't fly low if the swing doesn't finish low. The club should stop at shoulder height and be pointing at your target. If you swing any higher, you've probably used too much wrist or leg action. A higher finish also means a higher shot—and a loss of control.

SPIN IT BACK!

At a clinic, the seasoned pro took a question.

"When I hit my 7-iron, why doesn't the ball hit the green, bounce once, then spin backwards?" asked an elderly gentleman.

"Sir," responded the pro, "how far do you hit your 7-iron?"

"About 100 yards."

"Then why do you want it to come back?"

This oft-repeated story makes a good point: Most players shouldn't worry about imparting backspin on their shots.

However, there are times when sucking the ball back makes sense, particularly when the hole is cut at the front of the green just beyond trouble. Then it's great to be able to shoot for the fat of the green knowing the ball will come back. Here's how to do it.

1. A clean lie. The ball must be sitting up in the fairway so you can make a descending swing: You can't spin the ball with the sweeping swing you use off hardpan. From the rough, grass gets between clubface and ball, reducing the friction produced at impact. It's this friction that starts the ball spinning and explains why it's almost impossible to make a shot from rough "bite."

2. The right club. Don't expect spin from any club longer than a 7-iron. More-lofted clubs launch the ball higher, so the most spin comes off short irons and wedges.

3. The right kind of ball. A ball with a softer cover—either balata or one of the soft synthetics—spins faster than most Surlyn-covered balls. Also, a traditional three-piece (or wound) ball spins faster than most two-piece balls, although new technology has given the so-called "long-distance" balls more spin, and the latest generation of multi-layer balls are designed for both spin and distance. As a ball compresses against the clubface at impact, friction increases.

With the right conditions and equipment, play the ball back in your stance, as far back as off the instep of the right foot. The ball-back position encourages a steep swing and sharp downward blow.

Make a short, controlled backswing and keep the wrists firm.

Swing down hard, wrists firm, driving the legs toward the target. Hit down on the ball, "pinching" it against the clubface and ground. Don't help the ball into the air.

If you hit down crisply, the ball should fly high, bounce once or twice, then draw back. The faster and firmer your swing, the more the ball spins.

TROUBLE PLAY

Taming the Rough

How to Cope on a Slope

In Trouble in Trees

Lousy Lies

How to Handle Hardpan

Win When Wet

Wedge from Water

Long Distance from Long Rough

Win in the Wind

TAMING THE ROUGH

Unless all your shots travel the perfect line and distance, eventually you'll find the rough. Unlike the mown grass of fairways and greens, rough can be long and shaggy, sometimes making it hard to find, let alone hit, your ball.

Because the ball can sink into long grass, you can't rely on a standard technique to get free. You must change your swing to tame the rough stuff.

Whenever you're in the rough, assess the lie carefully. Is the ball sitting high or has it dropped into the jungle? If it's up, you may be able to take a long iron or wood and swing normally. But usually the ball falls at least some of the way down, so your only play might be nothing more than taking a short iron and blasting into the fairway. Your primary concern is to get out, even if you advance the ball only a few yards.

Having selected a club, set the clubface square, play the ball in the middle of your stance, and choke down on the grip. Hover the club above the grass until you swing; pushing it down may make the ball fall deeper. Make a steep swing so the clubface encounters limited resistance from the grass. However, some grass will wrap around the club on the downswing, closing the face so the ball flies left; aim slightly right at address to compensate.

Swing hard, but don't bring the hands back higher than the shoulders; the shortened swing helps maintain balance.

Balls coming out of rough tend to be "hot": Grass getting between club and ball at impact decreases spin, so shots fly lower than normal and roll after landing—from wet rough the ball flies even hotter. Plan accordingly.

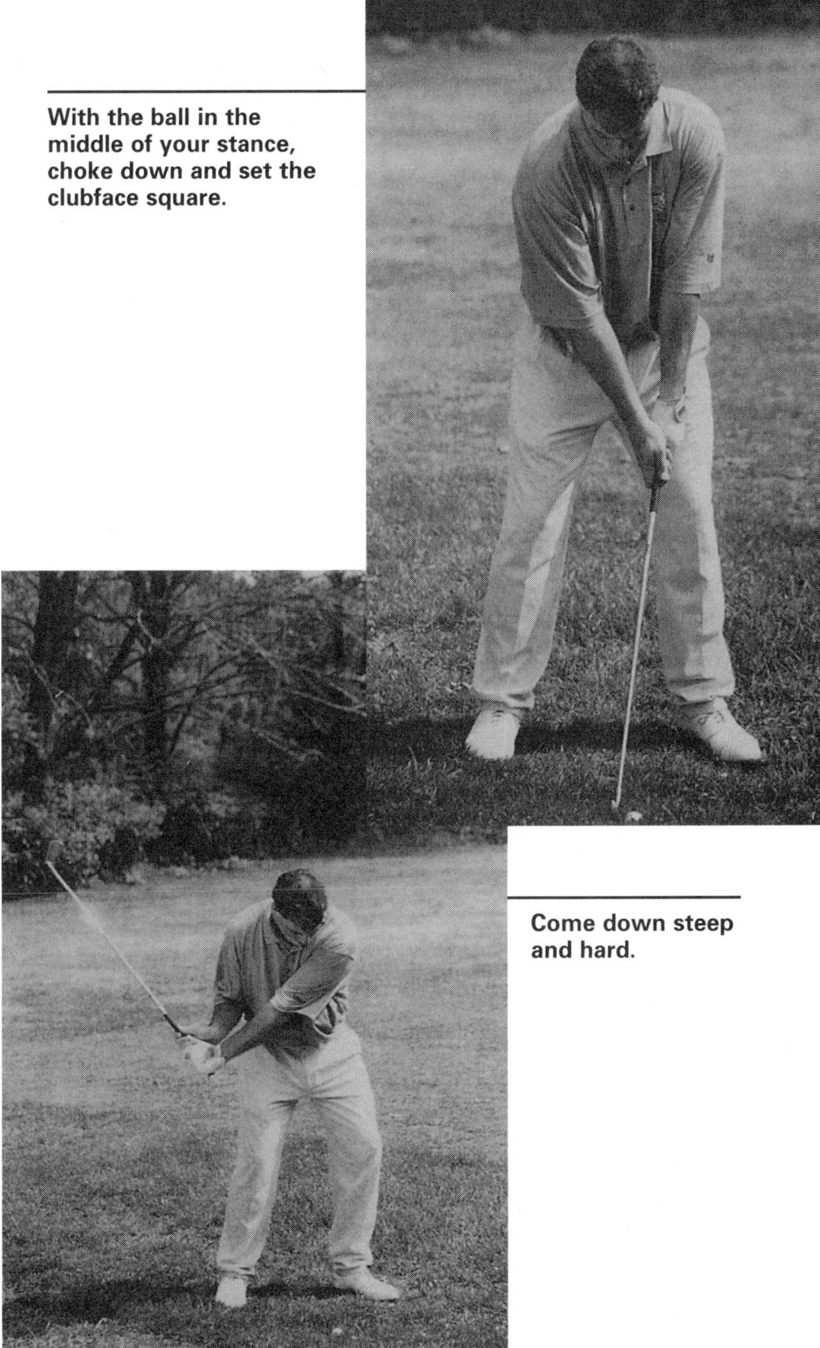

With the ball in the middle of your stance, choke down and set the clubface square.

Come down steep and hard.

Should your ball find greenside rough, play the shot like an explosion from sand. Using a sand wedge, open your stance (aiming shoulders, hips, and feet left of your target), play the ball forward in your stance, and make a wide, U-shaped swing. Hit behind the ball so it pops up and out; hitting too close launches a hot shot sure to fly the green.

HOW TO COPE ON A SLOPE

Despite your best intentions, the golf ball doesn't always settle on level ground. Eventually you'll have to hit off a hilly lie—the ball above your feet, below your feet, on an upslope, or on a downslope.

Playing off a hill requires proper balance, club selection, and ball flight. Here's how to make the grade from any grade.

UPHILL/DOWNHILL LIES

To make a good swing and maintain your balance, set your hips and shoulders parallel to the slope. On an uphill lie that means moving your back foot (the right foot for a right-hander) slightly down the hill; on a downhill lie, reposition the forward (left) foot down the hill. In both cases, take your stance so the ball is closer to the higher foot (left on an uphill lie, right on downhill).

Swing the club along the angle of the hill. The steeper the incline, the easier it is to lose balance, so make a shorter-than-normal swing.

Slope also influences the height and distance of shots, making club selection crucial. An uphill lie adds loft to the club so the ball flies higher and not as far; compensate by taking a club with less loft (for example, hit a 5- or 6-iron from your usual 7-iron distance). Reverse the procedure from a downhill lie, where you need a more-lofted club. Finally, resist the temptation to help the ball into the air off a downhill lie; the club can do it.

SIDEHILL LIES

A ball above or below the feet demands altering your posture, with the lie dictating how to stand. A ball above the feet is closer to your hands,

Uphill lie: Move your back foot farther back.

Downhill lie: Move your front foot farther down the slope.

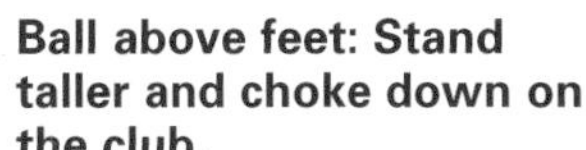

Ball above feet: Stand taller and choke down on the club.

Ball below feet: Bend more at the knees and hips.

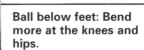

forcing you to stand taller but also flattening your swing (the club moves more around the body); conversely, a ball below your feet is farther away, forcing you to bend more to reach it (and creating a more up-and-down swing).

The changes to the swing influence ball flight. The flatter swing produced when the ball is above the feet means the shot will curve right to left; allow for the draw by aiming to the right.

The steeper swing caused by a ball below the feet creates a left-to-right pattern; aim left at address to handle that fade.

IN TROUBLE IN TREES

Golfers have a saying: "Trees are 90 percent air." That's true if you're trying to hit over or through them. But when your ball is under low-hanging branches, lying against roots, or situated so you can't make a normal swing, trees are 100 percent trouble.

From any lousy lie, you want to get the ball in the fairway with a chance of saving the hole. The following plays will help.

UNDER LOW BRANCHES

When limbs restrict your backswing, make several slow, smooth practice swings, bringing the club back until it just brushes the obstruction. When making the shot, stay slow and relaxed: Take the club as far back as you can, then swing with the arms and hands, keeping head and body still.

ROOT WORK

A ball against roots may be better left unplayed: There's no point breaking a club or your wrists. But sometimes you can safely get free.

If the ball is just in front of a root, top it with your putter. Choke down for control, swing easily, and hit the top of the ball.

If the ball is behind a root, be careful. The shot might bounce back, and if it touches you, it's a two-stroke penalty (to say nothing of potential injury). But if you have room, take a wedge and make an easy swing.

When a root is to the side of the ball away from you, stand a little further away, tighten your grip, and try making contact off the toe of the club.

If the root is between you and the ball, use your putter, or else turn around and use an inverted wedge, as described below.

UP AGAINST THE TRUNK

When you can't make a normal right-handed swing—thanks to roots or the trunk—turn yourself and your club around and play lefty.

Reverse your grip so the left hand is below the right. Set up square, make a smooth swing with the arms and hands, and keep your body still. Choose a club based on its features: The wedge has the largest head, whereas the flat backside of a long iron or putter provides the most roll.

Rooting around in the roots? Play it safe by topping the ball with your putter.

If you can't make a normal swing, turn the club over, reverse your grip, and swing easy to make good contact.

LOUSY LIES

Even a good course can present you with bad lies, spots where the grass isn't perfect, or isn't grass at all. Here's how to handle three common "lousy" situations.

IN THE MUD

The recovery from muck isn't difficult. Properly played, your biggest worry will be staying clean.

If the ball sits on top of the mud, address it as you would a fairway bunker shot: Position it back in your stance about an inch, and stand taller than usual. Swing easy, especially if your footing is slippery.

Play a plugged lie in the mud as you would one in the sand. Use your pitching wedge or a short iron, but not the sand wedge (the big flange will stick, rather than get through, the muck). Close the face a bit, open your stance, take a firm grip, and hit down on the ball. The deeper it's buried, the shorter it will fly, so plan accordingly.

DIVOT HOLE

Nothing is more frustrating than hitting a good drive only to find it in a divot hole in the fairway. Before planning the shot, calm down: Anger only produces tension.

Take an iron (a wood probably will snag), and set up for a normal shot with these changes:

The face should be square to slightly closed, whereas your swing has to be steeper than usual.

Because the ball is below the level of the fairway, you have to go down after it. Make a slow backswing, get set at the top (resist the temp-

Even a good shot can find a divot hole.

Make a slow, steady backswing, then swing down hard to dig the ball out.

tation to rush the downswing), and hit down hard. The ball will fly lower than usual, then roll after landing, so overall distance should be about normal for the club.

PERCHED LIE

When the ball sits up in a clump of long grass, be careful not to move it as you position the clubhead (that's a penalty). Then think about putting the clubhead on the ball rather than whiffing by passing under it.

Stand taller than normal and, if necessary, choke down on the club. For control, keep your backswing short, no more than halfway back. Make a shallow downswing, "sweeping" the ball of the grass rather than hitting down.

Again, swing easy. Worry about making clean contact, not achieving great distance.

HOW TO HANDLE HARDPAN

We like to think of golf courses as lush, green meadows of grass, but all too often we find a spot where the sprinklers don't reach or the maintenance crew has yet to tread.

One such area is hardpan, a catchall term for any grassless patch of hard ground, often made firmer from hours baking in the summer sun. Hardpan turns up in the rough, along cart paths, and in well-trod areas (around water fountains, benches, and so on). Unless the bald spot is marked as ground under repair (check on the scorecard or in the pro shop before the round), you have to play your ball where it lays. To do so involves altering your technique.

Better players can try sweeping the ball off hardpan, going for extra distance by using a long iron (but never a fairway wood). Play the ball up in your stance, almost off your left heel, and straighten up slightly by reducing the bend at your knees and waist. Make a slow, controlled swing, being careful not to shift your body position.

A tall stance and controlled swing are important because you must catch the ball cleanly, without hitting the ground first. If the club hits the hard spot, it will bounce up and top the ball.

The safer shot off hardpan is the trap. Play the ball in the center of your stance, open your alignment slightly (aiming left of target), and make a steep, three-quarter-length swing. On the downswing, keep a firm grip to hold the clubface a tad open at impact. Aim for the back of the ball, trapping it between the club and the ground. This shot offers a greater margin for error than the sweep, but you still must guard against topping.

Here's the safe shot off a hard, bare patch: Ball in middle of stance; make a steep, three-quarter swing.

Playing the ball back in your stance means the shot will fly lower and roll farther than normal. So take less club (e.g., a 9-iron from 8-iron distance).

Sweeping or trapping, the absence of grass exaggerates your chance of hooking and slicing. Should the club hit the ground first, it will twist, adding even more curve.

Remember: Make a slow, controlled swing and hit the ball before you hit the ground.

WIN WHEN WET

Golf is hard enough in good weather; rain only makes it more difficult. But you can still play well and have fun if you take the elements into consideration.

CLUB SELECTION

From the tee, think accuracy, not distance. Wet fairways will reduce roll, but more important, you want to avoid the rough, which becomes even more unmanageable when wet. So trade the driver for a 3-wood. That's also smart because water on the clubface or ball reduces spin, making shots fly low and dive to the ground; the 3-wood gives more air time.

On approaches, remember this rainy rule: Take more club for long shots, less for short shots.

On long shots, widen your stance and shorten your swing for stability, then take one more club to compensate for the distance lost to a three-quarter motion. Also try making a sweeping, rather than up-and-down, swing.

On short shots, when you're hitting either into the ground or through long grass, the moisture that gets between club and ball can cause a flier, a shot that comes out hot. Use a more-lofted club for control.

STRATEGY

Besides staying clear of rough, don't try to maneuver the ball; wet conditions make shotmaking unreliable, so your attempted fade could become a big banana.

Sand usually packs together when wet, so try chipping or even putting out. If you must explode, use a pitching wedge or 9-iron, which won't bounce off hard sand, and hit closer to the ball.

Check the greens before putting. If the rain has just begun, a film of water on top of the grass will make the ball run long. But once the rain soaks in, greens slow down and break has less effect.

GEAR

The key word is dry. Bring extra towels to wipe hands and grips. Change gloves often (special rain gloves are available). If you're still having trouble, swing with a handkerchief wrapped around the grip for traction.

The following are essential if you regularly play in rain: waterproof shoes, rain hat (with long bill if you wear glasses), rain suit, hood to protect clubs, umbrella.

Finally, beware of lightning. Walking on wet grass carrying metal rods makes golfers easy targets. At the first sign of a storm, get off the course or find a grounded rain shelter.

WEDGE FROM WATER

Hit your ball into trees, sand, or long grass and you'll likely find it and have a chance at recovery. A shot that finds the water, however, is almost certainly a stroke (and ball) lost.

Yet, if you find your ball by the edge of a stream or pond and the conditions are right, you can splash back in play without the burden of a penalty stroke. Here are the when and how of wedging out of water.

WHEN

Don't try this shot unless part of the ball is above the water. Many pros won't attempt this shot unless at least half the ball is above the surface. They know that a penalty stroke coupled with the opportunity to hit from dry land almost always prove the wiser choice.

HOW

Hitting from water requires a hard swing, so be sure you can take a solid stance. If more than one foot has to be in the water, you probably can't remain stable enough to pull this off.

Still want to play it?

Set up as if you're facing a buried lie in the sand. Take your pitching wedge (not the sand wedge, unless it has a sharp leading edge and no bounce) and close the face; this will compensate for the force of impact with the water, which will open the face slightly.

Bring the club up quickly by breaking the wrists in the backswing. Coming down, pull hard, aiming for a spot about an inch behind the ball. Don't quit on the swing: Unless you're committed to finishing this shot, the ball will stay in the water and you'll have to try all over again.

FINAL THOUGHTS

You're going to get wet, so don't flinch before impact. If you have a rain suit in your bag, put it on. If not, consider your clothes (and have a dry towel handy).

Water is a hazard, which means you can't touch it with the club before making your swing.

You're using a pitching or sand wedge, so don't expect more than 100 yards—and likely less—from this shot. If you manage to get out of the water at all, consider yourself lucky.

If you're uncomfortable with any of these facts, play smart: Take the penalty stroke and take your next shot from dry land.

LONG DISTANCE FROM LONG ROUGH

In summer, most golf courses share a common hazard: long rough. The thick, wiry grass that borders many fairways can gobble up off-line shots, often leaving nothing more than a pitch back to the fairway. But under the right conditions and with the right club, you can get good distance from the "spinach."

FAIRWAY WOOD

If the grass isn't too long and the ball hasn't fallen too deep, you can make clean contact with a well-lofted fairway wood, such as a 4-, 5-, 7- or 9-wood.

Open your stance (aim slightly left of target), and center the ball between your feet. Swing parallel to your body, taking the club on a steeper, out-to-in path. Don't drag the club through the rough on the takeaway: Lift it up quickly to minimize tangling in the grass.

As you come down, don't try to slug the ball. Stay smooth to ensure a solid hit. But don't quit on the shot, either: Use your strength to get through the grass. The combination of stance and swing creates a shot that flies high and lands soft starting left of the target and curving back to the right.

LONG IRON

When the grass isn't too long or the ball is sitting up, you can make a long shot with a long iron. A 3-, 4-, or 5-iron should be able to work through the rough and catch the ball cleanly.

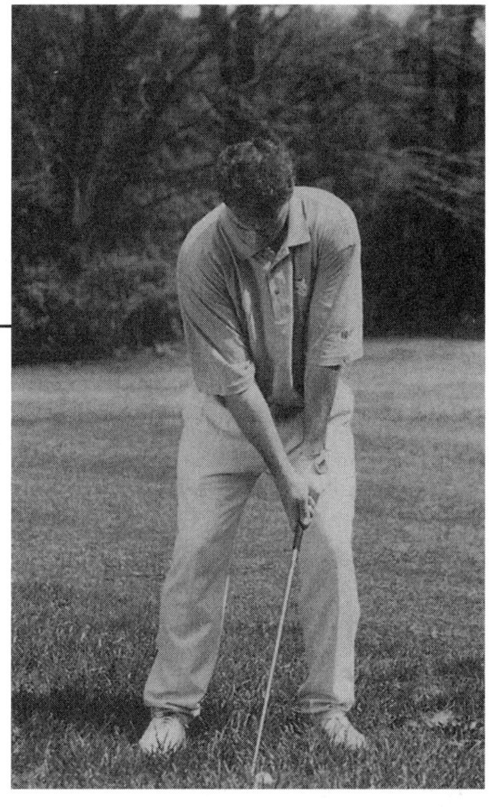

The smart play is to use an iron and play the ball from the middle of your stance.

Again, play the ball in the middle of your stance and aim left of your target; your cut shot will begin to the left, then curve right. The smaller head of the iron is susceptible to twisting and tangling as it meets the grass, so take a firm grip and pull the club into impact. Strive for a full finish.

The deeper the ball is in the grass, the steeper your swing. At some point, you won't be able to use anything longer than a short iron (8-, 9-, or wedge). That's when you must lift the club almost straight up and chop down on the ball with the simple intention of getting back into play. But again, hold tight and swing smoothly. Aim for a safe landing area, with plenty of room should the ball come out hot.

WIN IN THE WIND

Golf began in Scotland, on land near the sea. Consequently, golfers have long had to contend with the wind. There's even a Scottish expression, "If there's nae wind, there's nae golf."

In America, where most course are inland, wind is only an occasional factor, and many players don't know how to manage it. Some simple strategies will help you battle the breezes.

Shots will be affected by gusts over 10 miles per hour. Hitting into a headwind, your ball loses yardage. Into a tailwind, the ball flies farther, then runs after landing. Crosswinds can move the ball well off your intended line. So when it's gusty, plan your shots carefully.

Facing a headwind, take one extra club for every 10 mph of draft: If you usually hit a 7-iron 150 yards, you'll need a 4-iron when hitting into 30-mph gusts. Resist the impulse to swing harder; make a slow, three-quarter swing (the hands rising only to shoulder height). Finally, a headwind exaggerates a shot's bend: If your normal shot flies left to right, a headwind will move it farther right, so aim more to the left.

Tailwinds straighten out curve balls, so don't aim so far away from the target. Take less club, because not only does a tailwind keep the shot in the air longer, it brings the ball down on a shallower angle so it rolls after landing.

Ride a crosswind. Into a left-to-right gust, start your shot well to the left and let the wind bring it back. Aim five yards off the target for every 10 mph of breeze.

In any kind of wind, try a low-flying "knockdown" shot when hitting from the fairway. Take a club or two more than the distance dictates, and set up open—your feet and body aimed slightly to the left. Play the ball back in your stance (almost in line with the right heel), with the hands angled forward. Choke down on the club and keep a firm grip. Swing slowly to shoulder-height, then pull down and through with your left arm and hand. Restrict your follow-through so you finish with the club pointing at your target.

SHORT GAME

Chipping Made Easy

Love the Lob

The Versatile Putter

Do the Bump

CHIPPING MADE EASY

Every golfer should be able to chip. The stroke is short, the setup is simple, and the shot is used close to the green. So why do so many amateurs chip so poorly?

Because rather than thinking of the chip as a unique situation, they play it as a cross between a putt and a pitch, mixing the methods for those shots. The result is a jerky stab at the ball, which may or may not go straight and finishes way long or short of the hole.

The following chipping method is taught by short-game guru Dave Pelz, who works with many touring pros and has conducted extensive research on all parts of the game.

THE SETUP

Standing tall with your feet close together, play the ball well back in your stance—in line with the right ankle. Stand close to the ball so the club is almost vertical and the hands are raised; this helps the left hand and wrist stay firm.

Put most of your weight on your forward foot to encourage a descending blow. This also moves the hands forward, up to your left thigh. Because the ball is back in your stance, the club will be slightly open at impact: Close the clubface so it's square to the target line or aim left of your target.

THE SWING

The left arm does all the work as you make a smooth swing. Keep the lower body quiet. The backswing should be about 20 percent shorter

Feet close together, ball way back in the stance. The hands begin ahead of the ball and must lead the clubhead through impact.

than the follow-through to ensure acceleration through impact. (Most golfers do the opposite, swinging too far back, then decelerating on the downswing. This leads to inconsistent chips.)

Because this is a descending blow, you want to hit the little ball (the golf ball) before you hit the big ball (the ground).

STRATEGY

Practice chipping with all clubs from 5-iron through the wedges. The lower the loft, the lower the trajectory: Use lower-lofted clubs as you near the green so the ball lands on the surface quickly and rolls to the hole like a putt.

Aim for a spot about three feet onto the green. This compensates for the occasional mis-hit, getting the ball onto the green rather than leaving it in the long grass.

For consistency, the clubhead must be square at impact. An open or closed face reduces your control of distance and accuracy.

LOVE THE LOB

Trying to copy the pros often gets amateurs in trouble. But one shot the top players have that anyone can master is the high, soft floater that hits the green and stops.

The "lob" or "flop" shot is vital to the pro's game because he or she often plays on courses featuring long rough, diabolically placed bunkers, and humps that guard the green. You might not face trouble quite so severe, but if you've ever wanted to toss the ball high over a trap to a flagstick sitting near the edge of the green, you know the lob can be a lifesaver.

The lob is within the capability of all amateurs. What separates the greats from the rest of us is hours of practice, which not only hones their skills, but builds their confidence.

Here are two ways to hit the lob: Try them both, then perfect the one you like best.

1. Take a narrow, open stance with the ball played off your left heel. Use your sand wedge, with the face well open.

Make a slow, rhythmic backswing, cocking the wrists quickly in the takeaway. Don't decelerate coming down—drive through the ball.

2. Take the same setup: narrow, open stance, ball forward, open sand wedge. But instead of cocking the wrists quickly on the backswing, take the club back slow and low. Maintain an even tempo on the downswing and try to slide the bottom of the club under the ball. Don't let the right hand roll over, but let the left hand feel as if it's holding the clubface open through impact. In the follow-through, the clubface should point to the sky.

With a narrow stance, set your body open—pointing left of the target. Keep your head down as you swing through.

Both shots will do the job if there is at least a little grass under the ball. From long rough, the first shot, with the steeper blow, is less likely to let the club get tangled in the rough. If you're on a bare, hardpan lie, forget it: Neither technique will let you slide the clubface under the ball.

Both shots need a full swing, the club accelerating into and through impact. Practice to determine the distance and height produced by different lengths of backswing. The extra practice also will build confidence—just like the pros'.

THE VERSATILE PUTTER

One of the most versatile weapons in your bag is the putter, which has uses off the green as well as on. Practice first, then try these unusual shots with the flatstick.

THE TEXAS WEDGE

When you're off the green and there's nothing but short grass between the ball and the hole, consider putting—from as far as 50 feet away. The "Texas Wedge," so-called because it is popular on the hard, sun-baked fairways of the Southwest, works when you can't slide a wedge under the ball and there's no long grass to slow a putt's progress.

Take your putting stance and remain steady during the stroke. Make a long, smooth backstroke, accelerating through the ball into a full follow-through.

UNDER THE TREES

Nothing is more frustrating than finding your ball under branches that restrict your backswing. But a putter can give you good distance from this tough spot.

Settle in over the ball (even if your upper body is among the branches), spread your feet an extra 10 inches apart, and play the ball from the middle of your stance. Grip well down the shaft, bend at the waist, and swing the hands and arms, hitting hard into the back of the ball.

NO-LIP BUNKER

If you're in a greenside bunker that features firm sand and no lip, play the ball from the center of your stance and putt normally, stroking a little

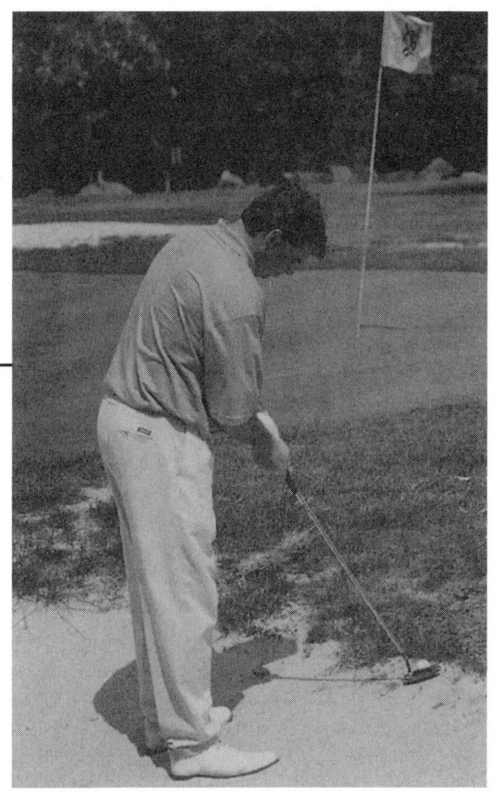

Have you ever thought of putting from a bunker? It's a smart, safe play when there's no lip in the way.

harder than for an on-the-green putt of the same distance. You also might try putting over a small lip, but be prepared for the ball to jump, then stop quickly on the green, making this a smart shot when the pin is tight.

UNDER THE LIP

This shot could only come from the Champions Tour's star Chi Chi Rodriguez, a true wizard from the sand. When he's buried under the lip of a greenside bunker, Chi Chi turns his putter 90 degrees and "knifes" the ball out with the toe of the club. (This works best with a thin, blade-type putter.)

Aim the toe at a spot behind the ball and set up open. Make a very steep swing, coming down hard so the toe makes contact half an inch behind the ball: Hit any closer and the ball will fly over the green; hit too far away and the ball won't escape the trap.

DO THE BUMP

The good golfer doesn't only shoot low scores but is creative, knowing more than one way to handle an unusual or difficult situation. Creativity is especially valuable within 60 yards of the green, the area pros call the "scoring zone."

In this zone, many amateurs automatically grab a wedge and try flying the ball to the hole. This shot puts them at the mercy of the wind, the green, and the pin position. If they played a low run-up or "bump and run," hitting the ball low and letting it run to the hole, their control would improve.

The run-up is the smart play when there's no hazard between you and the green and the ground is relatively flat. If the pin is on the far side of the green, use a club with just enough loft to drop the ball on the near side—perhaps as low as a 4- or 5-iron—so it rolls the rest of the way.

If the flag is close to you, choose a club that will let you land the ball a few yards short of the green, bounce once or twice, then roll on.

The technique is the same for both shots. The stance is narrow and slightly open (feet, hips, and shoulders aimed left of the target). Angle your hands ahead of the ball to encourage a descending blow. Swing with the arms, holding the wrists firm. Swing easy, keeping your head down so you don't lift up and hit the ball thin.

Practice with different clubs and lengths of swing to see how far—and how high—the ball flies. You may prefer one or two clubs, so hone your stroke with them, making longer and shorter swings and gauging distances.

The "bump" is a long chip shot. Place your feet almost together, set up open, and push your hands ahead of the ball.

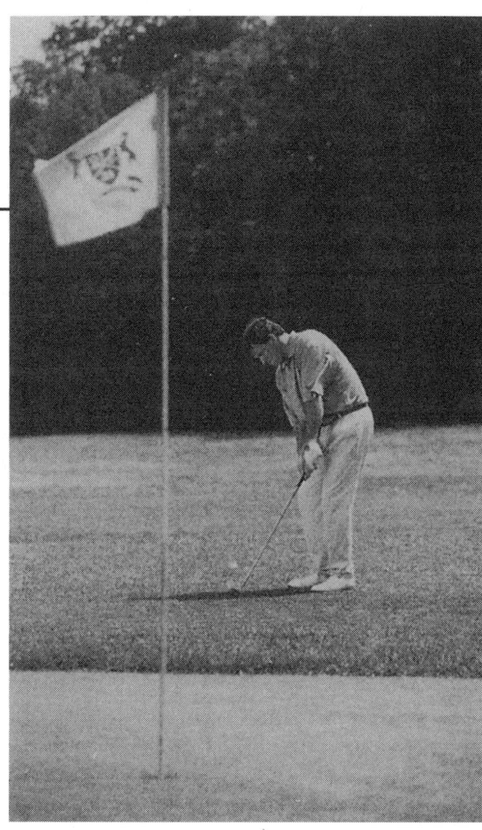

You also can use this shot when hitting to an elevated green with the pin close to you. Bump the ball into the slope just short of the green, letting it hop up and trickle on to the putting surface. Again, practice this shot first.

Finally, don't use the "bump" or run-up through long grass or on wet ground, both of which will kill the shot's momentum. In those conditions, take a wedge and loft the ball to the hole.

PUTTING

Two Putts Are Always Enough

Find—and Use—the Sweetspot

Read Any Good Greens Lately?

Peculiar Putting

TWO PUTTS ARE ALWAYS ENOUGH

A ball on the green doesn't mean you should expect to make your first putt. If you're 30 feet or more from the hole, you'll probably need two putts to get down. But if two putts are sufficient, any more than two are wasted strokes.

On long putts, most golfers do a good job controlling direction—reading the break and keeping the ball on line. Where amateurs have trouble is distance: They usually leave the ball well short or run it well past the hole.

To find the right range, start by aiming at a realistic target. The hole is only 4¼ inches across, almost impossible to see when you're 50 feet away. Rather than aiming for the hole try to stop the ball within a six-foot circle around the hole. What will be left is no more than a three-foot putt.

Next, check the surface. If the green runs uphill, you'll need a firmer stroke. If it's downhill, less stroke is necessary. Take a few practice strokes to get a feel for the distance.

Don't worry too much about sidehill slope in the first half of a long putt; the ball will be rolling pretty quickly so the break will have less effect. If there is break to contend with, aim the clubhead at the spot where it begins and set your body square to that target line.

The great Bobby Jones said the backstroke for a long putt should be "long enough." In other words, don't cut short the backstroke and then have to rush the forward stroke to compensate. Swing with the big muscles of the arms and shoulders, keeping them relaxed so the wrists can hinge naturally.

On a long putt, make sure your swing is long enough. Don't cut it short.

Make a smooth stroke. The length of the follow-through should mirror the backswing. Again, the wrists should hinge naturally.

Practice long putts, varying the length and conditions but always aiming for a six-foot circle. Getting down in two will become a sure thing, and you may drop some one-putts as well.

FIND—AND USE—THE SWEETSPOT

Some problems on the green aren't caused by a faulty stroke, but by your putter.

Most golfers know to try making contact with the club's "sweetspot," so they address the ball off the little line painted along the top of the clubhead. Unfortunately, that mark may not be accurate. So rather than efficiently transmitting the energy of the stroke, the ball is hit off line or an incorrect distance. Only the true sweetspot will propel the ball perfectly.

Here's how to find your putter's sweetspot—and use it.

HOW TO FIND IT

Hold the grip of your putter lightly in one hand, between the thumb and forefinger. With the other hand, tap the face of the putter using a coin or pencil. Keep tapping until you find the spot that sounds and feels the most solid, and that moves the club without the head twisting or turning. That point is the sweetspot.

Mark the spot by putting a small piece of tape or drop of paint directly above it on the club's top line. You want to be able to see this mark at address.

Practice hitting the ball firmly off this spot. Your putts should feel pure, with the ball rolling straight and true.

WHEN TO USE IT

Now that you've located the sweetspot, you want to hit it on every putt, right? Yes, but with one notable exception.

To locate the sweetspot of your putter, tap the face with a pencil until the head moves straight back without twisting.

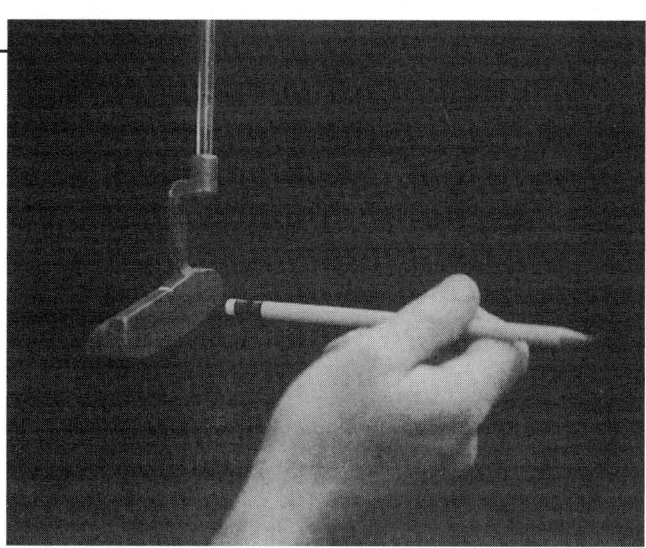

Deliberately missing the sweetspot is a clever way to handle fast and downhill greens. Think about it: If making contact with the sweetspot transmits the most energy, then missing it a little can throttle back your putting power. That can be just what you need when facing a speedy or sloping green.

In these cases, set up to hit the ball off the toe of your putter. Don't change your stroke; simply address the ball off the toe and make your normal motion. The ball will come off softer than if you hit it flush.

Practice this motion before taking it to the course. Because you're not hitting it flush, your "toed" putts may miss to the right. If so, slightly firm up your grip to keep the clubface from twisting open at impact.

READ ANY GOOD GREENS LATELY?

In the average round, nearly half your strokes will be putts. To lower your scores, learn to read greens for slope and grain, two factors that shape the path of a putt.

SLOPE

Most greens slope, tilting one direction or another, sometimes more than one at the same time. To determine how the land between your ball and the cup rises and falls, scope out the general contour of the green as you approach it from the fairway. On the green, check for slope from as many angles as prove necessary.

Start behind your ball and look toward the hole. This should be enough to judge the overall slope. Don't look too hard or you'll see a break that isn't there.

For more information, such as on a "double-breaker," look at the line of the putt from the low side of the hole, far enough away to see both the ball and hole at once. If you're still not sure, look from behind the hole back to the ball.

The more you look for slope, the more likely you are to become overloaded with information. If you learn to judge most putts with one look, you'll play faster and be less likely to "over-read."

GRAIN

This is the direction that grass grows. Like slope, grain influences a putt's speed and direction. A ball traveling with the grain rolls faster and breaks more sharply; a putt running into the grain moves more slowly and takes less break.

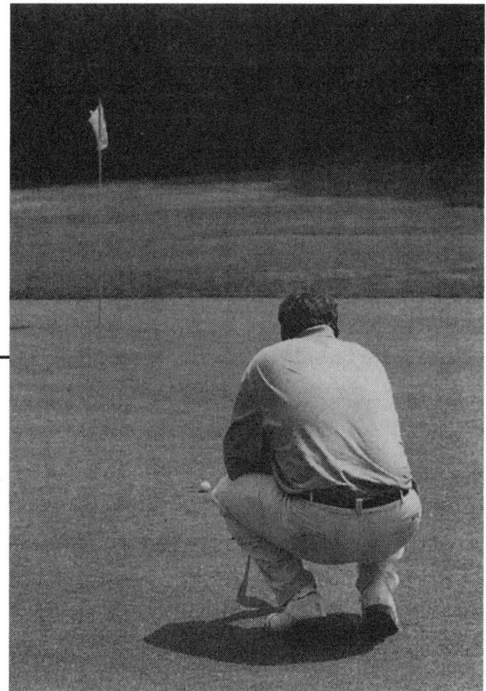

One good look from behind the ball to the hole should be enough to determine slope.

Look for grain when you make your first check for slope, from behind the ball toward the hole. If the grass appears shiny, you're putting with the grain; a dull finish indicates going against the grain.

Grain usually runs the same direction as the slope (since that's the way water runs off), but not always. To evaluate sidehill grain, look from the high side of the hole: Shiny grass means the grain indeed follows the slope, so the break will be exaggerated; no shine means putting into the grain and less break.

GENERAL RULES

Grain usually runs toward a body of water—ocean, river, lake—and away from bunkers.

Late in the day, grain runs toward the setting sun.

Grain is more prevalent on Bermuda grass, found in warm climates such as the South, less on bent grass. Remember that if you travel and play away from home.

PECULIAR PUTTING

If you watch golf on television, you may have noticed that while most Tour pros have smooth, simple swings, their putting strokes run the gamut from silky to silly. That's because putting is the most personal, and idiosyncratic, part of the game, where only one rule applies: If it works, it's good. What follows are descriptions of odd putting methods that work for four pros and might work for you.

LEE TREVINO

Trevino's putting stance resembles his full-swing position—feet and body aimed well left of the target. This gives him an unimpeded view of

Having trouble getting putts to the hole? "Jab" the ball...

Make a long backstroke...

both his line and the angle of the putter-head. To prevent pushing putts to the right from the open stance, Trevino takes the club straight back and through, while keeping his left wrist firm.

GARY PLAYER

If your putts, especially the little ones, come up short, Player's "jab" stroke may help. He takes a long backswing and accelerates coming forward, then stops the club immediately after impact. Putts roll with authority, which is useful on bumpy or shaggy greens, and on short putts when you want to eliminate the break. But be forewarned: It takes hours of practice to groove the jab, especially for long putts.

Cut the follow-through short.

CHI CHI RODRIGUEZ

One of the most colorful and entertaining players on the Champions Tour, Rodriguez is also one of its most consistent putters. His method is practically the opposite of Gary Player's: Chi Chi takes a very short backstroke, then drives through the ball, swinging the clubhead well past impact. Another interesting aspect of this stroke is its path—well to the inside going back, square at impact, then back to the inside on the follow-through. Like Player's, this method gives putts snap so that they bang into the cup. But again, be prepared to practice to make this technique effective.

DAVE RUMMELLS

This journeyman pro on the regular Tour stands so upright, you'd think he was using a long putter. But no, his flatstick is conventional length. Standing tall positions Rummells' eyes directly above the ball and gives him a clear view of the target line, two keys to good direction. An erect posture also encourages a straight-back, straight-through pendulum stroke, which all but guarantees a square putterface at impact.

SAND PLAY

Don't Be Scared of the Sand

Fairway Sand

Hard Sand, Soft Sand

Downhill in the Sand

Beating the Buried Lie

DON'T BE SCARED OF THE SAND

If you're like most golfers, you're scared of the sand. Because you dread being "on the beach," you're beaten even before trying to get out.

But sand play is not difficult. With practice and the proper fundamentals, you'll have no trouble getting from grit to green.

From a greenside bunker, use the sand wedge. It has a rounded flange on the bottom called the "bounce" that makes the club rebound upon contacting the sand.

To take advantage of the bounce, the club should hit the sand an inch or two behind the ball. The club will bounce, lifting out some sand and the ball. Remember: The club never hits the ball.

Set up with the ball forward, almost off your left heel. Open your stance, angling your feet and body so they point left of your target: The further left you aim, the higher and shorter the shot. For very short shots or when you have to get the ball up quickly (such as in a bunker with a steep lip), aim well left at address.

Twist your feet into the sand to build a solid foundation, but not so deep that your legs can't move.

Open the clubface, repositioning the club in your hands so the face points to the right of the target. Just as with an open stance, opening the clubface sends the ball higher and shorter. Practice combinations of open stance and open clubface to see how the ball reacts.

When the ball is sitting up on the sand, make a smooth, shallow swing and a full follow-through. If the ball is plugged—what golfers call a "fried egg"—aim the clubface at the target and make a steep swing, cocking the wrists early. On the downswing, knife the club into the sand behind the ball; there won't be any follow-through on this shot.

Play the ball forward off the heel, and open your stance.

If your ball is on a slope, set your shoulders and hips parallel to the hill. On an uphill lie, play the ball back in your stance; on a downhill lie, increase your knee flex and hit another inch farther behind the ball.

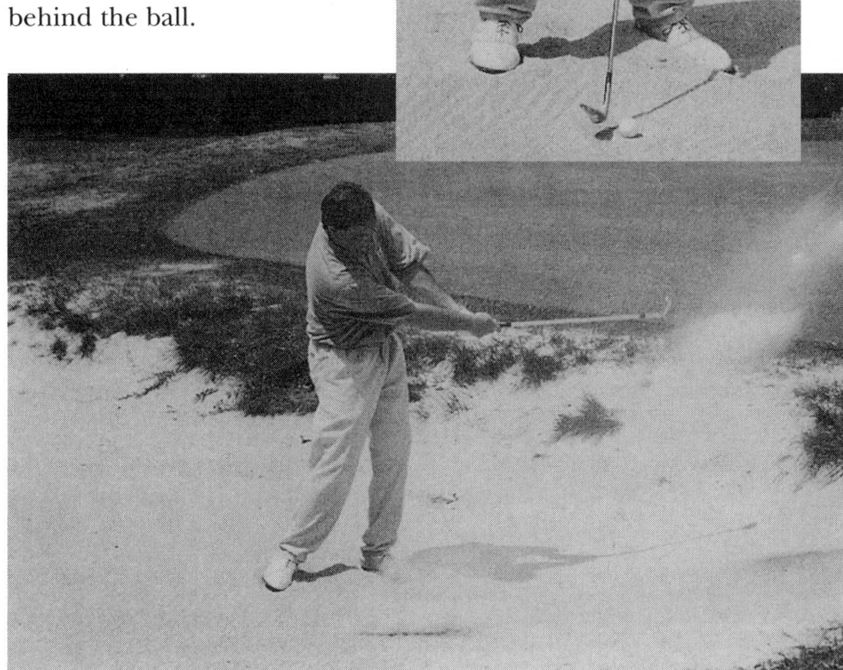

Then finish, swinging through the sand into a real follow-through.

FAIRWAY SAND

Fairway bunkers are usually placed where they can do the most damage: near the landing area for drives, on a dogleg, pinching short par-fours, and so on, which means you're likely to land in one eventually. The secrets to getting out are choosing the right club and swinging easy.

If your ball plugs in a fairway trap, take your sand wedge and take your medicine: Blast out as best you can. But if your ball is sitting up, you can use a long iron, even a wood, and get back in the hole.

Figure the distance to your target (the green or a lay-up spot) and pick the club that will reach it. Then check the lip of the bunker between you and your target: Can the club you chose fly the ball over that lip? Getting up and out is your first concern, so use a higher-lofted club if necessary, sacrificing distance.

In a fairway bunker, you want the club to hit the ball before it contacts sand. Position the ball an inch or two further back in your stance, choke down about half an inch, and plan to make a steeper-than-normal swing.

To keep your balance, create a solid foundation by twisting your feet into the sand; not as deep as for a greenside bunker shot, but enough that you won't sway during the swing. While digging in restricts lower-body movement, it also robs power: You'll need a less-lofted club to make up the lost distance; be sure there's still sufficient loft to clear the lip.

Swing primarily with the arms, letting the hands rise to shoulder height (a "three-quarter" swing). A shorter swing also helps keep the body from moving.

This technique works with woods as well as irons. The lofted woods—5 and higher—can work wonders from fairway bunkers: Widen your

Choose the club with enough loft to get the ball over the lip of the bunker.

stance an extra inch or two for stability, and concentrate on making a short, steep swing.

Finally, don't touch the sand with the club before you swing. Even a terrific shot won't make up the two-stroke penalty for grounding a club in a bunker.

HARD SAND, SOFT SAND

Most golfers have enough trouble escaping from greenside bunkers without worrying about different types of sand. But one reason the amateur leaves his ball in the trap—or skulls it over the green—is that he forgets to change both his club and swing for soft or hard sand. Here's what you should know. (Note: All these shots work only when the ball is sitting up on the sand or is only slightly embedded.)

STANDARD SAND

For the standard shot, use a standard sand wedge, one with neither too much nor too little "bounce"—that is, the angle that the flange hangs below the sole: The more the flange slopes down from the club's leading edge, the greater the bounce.

Dig your feet in slightly and open both your stance and the clubface. On the backswing, cock the wrists quickly; coming down, splash the clubhead into the sand about two inches behind the ball.

Vary the length of the swing for distance—a longer swing for longer shots, a shorter swing for less distance. However, no matter how big the swing, strive for a full follow-through. Don't decelerate on the downswing or the club will get stuck in the sand, as will the ball.

HARD SAND

Here you need a sand wedge with less bounce, so the sole is flat as on most other clubs. With little or no bounce, the leading edge contacts the sand first, digging in and under the ball. If you don't have a no-bounce sand wedge, try a pitching wedge.

Make the same swing as described above, but square the blade to the target and contact the sand a little closer to the ball. The shot will fly lower and run farther after hitting the green.

On very hard sand, like baked dirt or hardpan, pitch the ball out: Play it back in your stance, angle your hands ahead, and nip the ball off the surface.

SOFT SAND

In the fluffy stuff, a sand wedge with extra bounce—the sole protruding well below the leading edge—works best. The large flange helps the club slide through the sand, but only if you make contact about an inch behind the ball. Hit the sand too far back and the club will bounce up and strike the ball a glancing blow, sending it nowhere.

DOWNHILL IN THE SAND

Without question, one of the toughest shots in golf is the downhill lie in a bunker. As with any difficult shot, there is a proper way to play it. But most golfers are afraid of "blading" the ball, hitting it dead center with the leading edge of the club, skulling it across the green and off the far side. Once that thought gets in their heads, it usually becomes a self-fulfilling prophecy.

You can hit this shot successfully if you understand what it entails and how to compensate for the awkward lie.

STANCE

Because your feet are at different heights, building a solid foundation is important. Bend your back leg so your hips and shoulders are parallel to the slope. Twist your feet into the sand enough to feel secure, but not so much that you're no longer level with the ground. If your back foot is out of the bunker, be sure it is planted securely and won't twist or turn.

GRIP

To make the necessary wristy swing, grip lightly in the fingers. Choke down for control, almost to the bottom of the rubber.

SWING

Cock the wrists to begin backswing, and don't take the club any further than three-quarter height; more than that and you may lose your balance at the top. Make a controlled swing, resisting the temptation to rush and get it over with.

Flex your back leg to set hips and shoulders parallel to the slope of the bunker.

Coming down, keep your lower body still, swing firmly with the arms, and hit two to three inches behind the ball. Swing along the angle of the slope, taking a good cut of sand while trying to make a full finish. You probably won't be able to complete the follow-through, but trying encourages acceleration, which is crucial.

SPECIAL CASES

Sometimes you won't be able to make a steep enough swing, the ball will be buried, or for some other reason you lack confidence in the shot. Then take your medicine and play sideways or even backward. But don't give up on the hole. Think where you want to hit your next shot from and fight for that par or bogey, either of which is a respectable score from an impossible lie.

BEATING THE BURIED LIE

What could be worse than finding your ball in a bunker? Realizing that it's plugged, with only a little bit sticking out of the sand. The buried lie scares golfers because they don't know that all it takes is a change in technique and equipment to make getting out easy.

On a normal sand shot, when the ball sits on the sand you use a sand wedge, which has a big flange that slides through the grit. But with a buried lie the club has to dig into the sand to get down to the ball. So use your pitching wedge, which has no flange.

The basic sand shot is played with the ball forward in the stance to pop the ball up. For the plugged shot, center the ball between your feet, making it easier to drive the club into the sand.

Twist your feet into the sand a little more than usual, which helps lower the club to the level of the ball. Your feet and body can be either square or a little open (aiming left of the target), but the clubface must be square or even a little closed. Push most of your weight onto your front foot.

Make a very steep swing. Keep a firm grip as you bring the club up sharply with a quick wrist break, then pull down hard with the left arm, hitting the sand about two inches behind the ball. You have to move a lot of sand to drive the club down to the ball, so hit hard! The ball will come out in a cloud of sand, hit the green, and run a long way.

Chi Chi Rodriguez, who is a wizard from the sand, alters this technique slightly to make the ball sit quickly on the green. He sets up open to the target and opens the blade of his pitching wedge. He makes the same steep, wristy swing, but as the club knifes into the sand, he holds on tight to keep the face open through impact. The ball flies high, spins a little to the right after landing, then stops. Whichever shot you choose, both demand a hard hit, strong wrists, and plenty of practice.

Use a pitching wedge, play it square, and drive it into the sand just behind the ball.

STRATEGY

Tournament Tough

Conquer the Par-Threes

Safe, Smart Strategy

Vary Your Set

Cold Weather Play

When the Wheels Fall Off

Chart Your Progress

Mind Games

Let TV Teach You

Start the New Year Right

TOURNAMENT TOUGH

If you've ever played in a tournament, even the high-handicap flight at your club, you know that competition takes a toll. Suddenly even the simple shots are difficult, while your thoughts race by a mile a minute.

To perform your best in a championship, you must be prepared both physically and mentally. Here are some ways to get—and stay—tournament tough.

KNOW THE COURSE

Low handicapper or novice, get a look at the course before play begins (if you can get in a practice round, even better). You don't want to stand on a tee wondering what's over the hill. Good players may want to pace off yardages, check the sand, and test the greens for speed.

All players will want to know if an unfamiliar layout is tight or wide open, long or short, wet or dry. Once you know, be prepared for a particular type of play. Make a game plan and stick with it.

Competing on your regular course, prepare by playing each hole in your mind. Remember your greatest shots in every situation and bring a positive attitude to the first tee.

PRACTICE

Once you know what to expect, practice shots that will come in handy. Long courses demand fairway-wood and long-iron approaches plus a good short game. A tight course may take the driver out of your hands, so practice with its replacement. Know the shots you'll need and be able to hit them with confidence.

PLAY YOUR GAME

Once the round begins, stick to your game plan; don't let your opponent make you change it.

If you're competing against a long hitter, don't try to out-hit him. Concentrate on accuracy. You'll often hit first in the fairway: Turn that into an advantage by sticking the ball close, putting pressure on him.

Against a short hitter, don't swing for the fences every time or eventually you'll find trouble. Throttle back for control and accuracy.

STAY RELAXED

If you're playing well, don't get cocky; take it one shot at a time. Don't start writing a victory speech until you're done.

If you're playing poorly, chalk it up to experience. There will be a next time.

Finally, win or lose, be a good sport.

CONQUER THE PAR-THREES

Par-threes usually are considered the easiest holes on a golf course because they're the shortest. However, architects often compensate for lack of distance with a wealth of other trouble—such as hazards, small greens, and variations in elevation. So although only one shot is necessary to reach the green, it had better be a good one. Here's how to be sure it is.

Know the exact yardage. Don't go by the scorecard, but pace off the distance from a marked sprinkler head or sign to the tee blocks. Also know if yardages are to the middle or front of the green.

You can tee up as far as two clubs-lengths behind the blocks. That can make you more comfortable with club selection or guarantee a level lie.

Use a tee peg to encourage good contact. Teeing the ball higher than normal promotes a high shot, cutting a few yards off a club's normal distance. The cardinal rule of club selection is be safe. Look at the green: If the trouble is short (which is more common than hazards lurking behind a green), hit a little long.

Aim away from trouble, which usually means going for the fat of the green. Shooting at a pin tucked behind a bunker is a sucker play; better to face a long putt than an explosion from sand. If trouble sits all around a green, think about which second shot you prefer—for example, sand or rough—and aim away from the worst.

Whenever possible, play your natural shot. That might mean aiming away from the flag if it's on the left side and you hit a fade. But you don't want to try creating a shot when you're looking at trouble and a small green.

Teeing the ball higher promotes a higher, shorter shot.

Factor in the wind. Look at the flag and trees around the green for movement. Also consider the elevation: Take more club when hitting to an elevated green, less club to a green below the tee.

If you're between clubs, hit the longer one. A smooth swing with a 6-iron is smarter play trying to jump on a 7.

Finally, if the green is out of your range, aim for a bail-out area. But then, too, play a smart shot, positioning the ball so your next shot isn't over trouble.

SAFE, SMART STRATEGY

How do you play a hole? Do you stand on the tee, look down the fairway, then swing, simply hoping to put the ball out there "somewhere"? Do you not think about the next shot until you've seen where the last one lands? If so, you are wasting strokes.

Scratch player or hacker, you should approach each hole with a plan. Strategy is important for mastering a hole and lowering your score, and also can help you hit better shots by making you focus on the task at hand.

Here are two simple strategies every player should use.

PLAY BACK FROM THE HOLE

Rather than thinking first about your tee shot, start by seeing your approach. What—and from where—do you want to be hitting to the green?

If the flagstick is tucked on the right side behind a bunker, you probably want to shoot at it from the left, avoiding the sand and leaving the most green to work with. That means the shot before should finish on the left side of the fairway.

On most par-fives, you have to think two shots ahead to see your approach. Because par-fives usually have strategically placed hazards—fairway bunkers, water, and so on—you also must consider club selection. For example, a fairway-wood second shot travels the longest distance, but also may bring the trouble into play. Consider a long- or mid-iron lay-up to avoid those obstacles.

PLAY FOR THE FULL SHOT

Besides calculating position, figure out which club you want for your approach. You probably don't want a 50-yard half-wedge or some other finesse shot. The safer play is the 100-yard wedge or 9-iron, which lets you take a full swing.

Setting up the approach this way calls for knowing your yardages with every club. Not just the short irons you're hitting to the green, but the longer clubs as well.

If booming a driver 250 yards will leave you a 65-yard touch shot, you must know which club will carry 200 yards off the tee and leave the 115-yard full 9-iron. Is that your 5-wood? 2-iron? Know the distance for each club—and practice tee shots with all of them.

VARY YOUR SET

Although the Rules of Golf limit you to 14 clubs, that doesn't mean you can't own more. In fact, you should have at least 20, with "replacements" ready to go depending on the course and conditions you'll be facing. Here's how to mix and match clubs.

DRIVERS

On wide-open, hazard-free holes, try a driver with a longer shaft (45 to 47 inches) and less loft (8 to 10 degrees). This combination should produce longer shots while not sacrificing accuracy.

On tight holes, go with a standard shaft and a little more loft (10 to 12 degrees) for control. If accuracy remains a problem, tee off with one of your fairway woods, which are shorter and carry more loft.

FAIRWAY WOODS OR LONG IRONS?

Assuming you hit both equally well, you'll want to switch depending on the rough. From long grass, woods are more likely to cut through and make clean contact. "Trouble woods," with runners and angled soles, are especially helpful from long grass and fairway bunkers.

WEDGES

Your choice of sand wedge should be dictated by the bunkers. From hard, packed sand, you need very little "bounce"—the angle that the bottom of the clubhead drops below the leading edge; "very little" is less than 9 degrees, which also makes this a good club from tight fairway lies.

From average sand, use an average wedge, with 10 to 13 degrees of bounce. Soft sand demands more bounce, 14 degrees and up; this wedge also can handle fluffy greenside rough.

If you face high lobs and delicate shots over bunkers, consider a "third" wedge of 60 to 65 degrees. It will send the ball high but short, so be careful.

PUTTERS

On wet, slow (including Bermuda grass) greens, a heavy putter makes it easier to get the ball to the hole with your normal stroke. Dry, fast greens will succumb to a lighter putter that shouldn't drive the ball way past the cup.

If you have trouble with short putts, carry two putters—one regular length and one long. Use the standard putter everywhere except inside five feet. Then you should take the long putter, which encourages an erect stance and a straight-back, straight-through, wristless stroke. One caution: Practice with the long putter first; it takes getting used to.

COLD WEATHER PLAY

Just because cold winds are blowing and the ground is frozen, don't assume you won't play again until spring. You can enjoy late-autumn and winter golf by making some changes in your technique and attitude.

DRESS WISELY

First and foremost, dress warmly. Wear many layers, including long underwear, turtlenecks, sweaters, windbreakers, and other clothes that will keep you warm and the wind out, yet let you make the freest possible swing. Don't forget a hat (that covers the ears) and gloves; keeping hands and feet warm is vital to good play and good health.

Be sure to loosen up before teeing off. Muscles will be stiffer than in warm weather, which means a greater chance of injury. On the course, swing easy.

CHANGE BALLS

If you usually play a two-piece or 100-compression three-piece ball, cold weather impact can prove shocking and painful. Hard balls feel even harder in the cold weather, so you might try a 90-compression or extra-soft-cover two-piece ball. Warm extra balls by keeping one or two in your pocket, alternating them hole to hole.

CHANGE YOUR SWING

If you usually hit down and take a divot, you'll find that the frozen ground won't give, so your club bounces up and tops the ball. Alter your technique to make a more sweeping swing, playing the ball farther up in your stance and picking it cleanly off the turf. A sweeping swing also is easier on the hands.

Adjust your strategy as well. The cold, hard ground should produce more roll, but conditions will be poor, so you'll get odd bounces and lies. A higher shot hit with one more club will sit down faster.

Around the greens, play the chip-and-run (with a sweeping stroke) rather than trying to hit down and pinch the ball between club and ground for a high shot. The lower flight will produce a more consistent bounce than the high shot.

When putting, realize that greens aren't being mowed or kept in shape, so expect poor conditions and little control over distance and direction. Futhermore, frozen fingers don't offer much feel.

Don't take winter golf too seriously. Consider every round a bonus and try to have fun. And if it gets too cold, come inside.

WHEN THE WHEELS FALL OFF

You're playing well for a round, a week, or a month, when suddenly your game goes south. Instead of long, straight drives, the ball dribbles off the tee or slices uncontrollably. Crisp, high iron shots are replaced by fluffs and skulls, and your short game is a shank-fest.

What to do? Don't panic. Every player—from pro to high-handicapper—hits the skids sometimes. Deal intelligently with your troubles to get back on track.

DURING A ROUND

If you're playing fine for a few holes and then become a bumbling fool, stop worrying about the score and simply try to hit good shots. Choke down half an inch on each club while slowing your swing; these changes promote control. Work especially hard on your short game, which can keep a poor round from becoming disastrous.

AFTER THE ROUND

If you aren't too frustrated, go to the range and check the basics: grip, alignment, stance, ball position, tempo. Chances are your problem is with one of these.

Grip and alignment are especially likely culprits because small changes can be hard to notice, yet have great effect. Has the club moved from across the palm of your left hand into the fingers? Have you put so much emphasis on power that you're squeezing too tightly? Are you aiming the upper body one way and the legs another? Place clubs along your feet, thighs, hips, and shoulders to check alignment before every shot.

TAKE A BREAK

If you don't spot your fault immediately, stay away from the course for a few weeks (but don't stop practicing). The stress of trying to score—and compete in money matches—will only exaggerate your problems.

LOOK FOR THE REAL TROUBLE

You may think your whole game is a mess, when it's really only one part. For example, if your long irons go bad, that puts pressure on your tee shots for more distance and your short game and putting for saves, causing them to suffer. Once you fix the weak link, the other pieces will fall in line.

SEE A PRO

In your frustration, it can be impossible to spot a fault. Have a teaching pro look you over and make suggestions. Once repaired, go for regular checkups to ensure everything is running smoothly.

CHART YOUR PROGRESS

Not all improvement comes from swing changes, new shots, and extra yards off the tee. You can add control and confidence by knowing your game and your course. Charting how and where you play will provide insights that translate into lower scores.

CHART YOUR GAME

All it takes is a scorecard and a few seconds per hole to start seeing your strengths and weaknesses.

After every shot, jot down what club you hit, how far you hit it, and where it landed—right, left, fairway, rough, green, sand, and so on. (Devise a notation system so you can do this quickly.) On the green, don't simply count the number of putts but note the length so you know if you had a realistic chance.

After a few rounds, you'll start seeing trends. Look for strong and weak holes and find the differences: Does hitting the driver usually put you in the rough? Try the 3-wood or a long iron. Does a greenside trap force you to lay up, yet you still make par? Maybe you should play short on other holes. Do you regularly three-putt from more than 20 feet? A lesson could help.

It takes only a few minutes and a few rounds to provide hours of analysis.

CHART YOUR COURSE

If you play most of your golf on one course, you'd better know it well. One walk with a notebook can do the job.

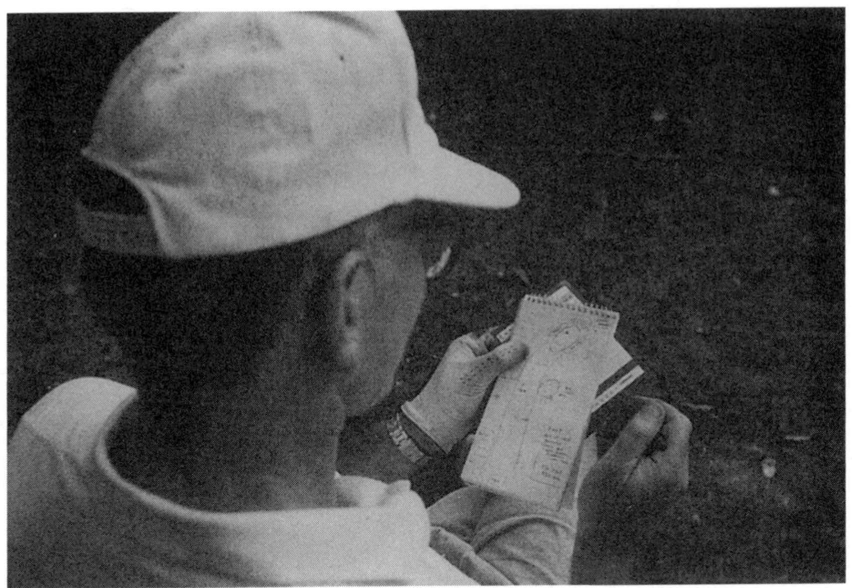

Make your own yardage book, noting the spots from where you usually play.

On a quiet afternoon, measure the course from where your shots usually land. It's especially important if you often find the same trouble: Know the precise yardage from under that tree to the green as well as to a safe lay-up spot.

Pace off the greens, back to front and side to side, so you have a sense of the yardage if the pin is forward or back. Also figure the extra yards necessary to carry a strategically placed bunker.

Note which greens are fast and slow and where the breaks are. This is important when hitting to a well-protected green: You don't want to be coming out of a bunker to a downhill green, so aim your approach well away from the sand.

Finally, periodically chart the yardage for each club—both carry alone and total yardage (including roll). Nothing builds confidence like knowing you can carry a pond with room to spare. But you'll only be sure if you know your distance with each club and the distance over the water.

MIND GAMES

Everybody's heard the expression "Golf is 90 percent mental." But many golfers don't know how to use their heads to help them play better. Here are a few basics of the "mental game."

WHO ARE YOU?

Are you a Jack Nicklaus type, capable of staying serious for the whole 18 holes? Or are you a Lee Trevino, laughing and thinking about other things? Figure out who you are on the course and don't try to be someone else. Use your strength—either intense concentration or the ability to "stop and smell the roses"—to your advantage.

MENTAL WARM-UP

Before going to the course, play the round in your mind. Sit in a chair and picture yourself hitting all the right shots. If there's one shot that regularly gives you trouble, play it over and over to yourself, imagining good results. You'll be prepared for success when you actually face the situation.

VISUALIZE

On the course, don't hit any shot without seeing it first in your mind's eye. Whether it's a drive soaring 240 yards down the middle or a three-foot putt dropping in the cup, picture your motion and the ball's motion before you make a move. Having pictured the results you want, your body will be better able to achieve them.

Play a round in your head before heading to the course. See each shot finding its target.

NO NEGATIVE THOUGHTS

Too often the last thought a golfer has before swinging is "I hope I don't hit it into the trees/water/sand/out of bounds." Holding a negative thought sets you up for a bad result. You want to keep your mind busy during the swing so negatives can't creep in. Timothy Gallwey, who wrote *The Inner Game of Golf,* suggests filling your mind by saying the word "back" to yourself as you bring the club back, then "hit" as you swing down to the ball. This exercise also helps slow your swing, another benefit.

DON'T OVERANALYZE

Although you need to consider the lie, wind, pin position, and other variables of a shot, don't overdo it. Don't strain your brain looking for subtleties that don't matter. Take a look, form a fast mental picture, then go to work. Keep it simple and your mind and body will work together.

LET TV TEACH YOU

If you're like most amateurs, you watch the pros—men, women, and seniors—on television battling for big money. However, if you're watching simply as a fan, you're missing the best lessons money can't buy. If you know what to watch for, you can pick up free pointers on shotmaking, strategy, course management, and more.

TEMPO

Watch how the stars swing within themselves. Every pro knows what his or her optimum tempo is, slow or fast, and tries to swing at that speed every

Every televised tournament can be like a free lesson from the world's best players.

time. It's when the rhythm changes that bad shots happen. Also watch how the pro's pace is evident in everything else—walking, setting up, putting.

TEMPER

A mental or physical mistake takes money out of a pro's pocket, so they're entitled to get mad after flubbing a shot. But once the steam is released, they're back to business: The bad shot is forgotten and their attention is turned to the shots to come.

PRACTICE SWING

It's very rare that a pro doesn't take at least one practice swing. He's trying to feel the proper motion and release a little tension. He's probably also envisioning a successful result to the shot in his head, programming his body to follow suit.

ON THE TEE

Watch where the pros tee it up—left, right, center, back and forth within the tee box. They use every allowable inch to give them the best angle to the fairway or green.

OUT OF TROUBLE

The cameras like to catch the miracle shot from trouble, but notice how often the pros take their medicine and chip back into the fairway to set up the next shot. They know that good scores follow from smart, safe play and that trying to be a hero can be dangerous.

ON THE GREENS

Amateurs shouldn't spend as much time as the pros do lining up putts from every angle. But notice that their putts are bold—they make it to the hole. Also note that on a breaking putt, pros usually miss above the hole rather than below it. This comes with a bold stroke since a weak attempt never has a chance to tame the break.

Something else about being bold: If the ball does run past the hole, you'll see how it will move coming back.

START THE NEW YEAR RIGHT

Another new golf season is beginning and you can't wait to step onto the first tee, pull the cover off your driver, and let fly. But before you take your first swing, take a good look at yourself and your game and make plans that will help make this your best year yet.

ANALYZE YOUR WEAKNESSES

Grab a pad and pencil, sit down, and think about last year's rounds. Here did you make your mistakes? What did your bad shots look like? Why did you get beat? Did you hurt yourself off the tee? On the greens? From the sand? Be honest, consider your weak points, and make a commitment to practice. Consider going to your pro for a lesson dedicated solely to these weak areas.

KNOW YOUR COURSE

Chances are you play most of your golf on the same course. So how well do you know it? Do you know where all the 150-yard markers are? Do you know which sides of the fairways set up the best approaches? Do you know how far it is to carry the bunkers, trees, or water? Walk your course early in the season with a pad and make notes that will help you all year long.

GET IN SHAPE

A few sit-sups, regular stretching, and swinging a weighted driver will help you be stronger, more flexible, and less prone to injury. Devise a routine and stick to it all year long.

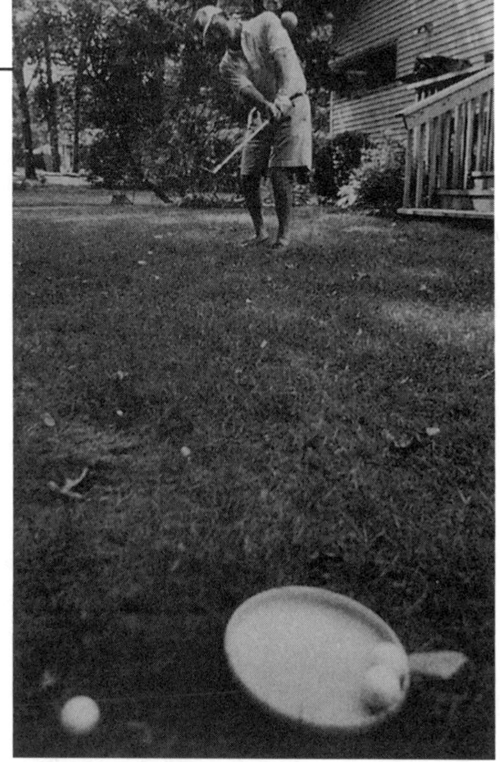

To keep your touch sharp, practice chipping in the backyard—or indoors—throughout the year.

WORK ON ALIGNMENT

A common problem for new players as well as old is aim, especially early in the year. Practice with clubs across your toes to be sure you're setting up square to the target. Get used to what proper alignment looks and feels like. Check yourself from time to time throughout the year, especially if you suddenly develop accuracy problems.

PRACTICE TOUCH

Chip in the backyard, putt on the carpet, practice hitting punches and other "escapes." Trouble shots and your skills on and around the green will save you strokes all year long, so don't neglect them.

CHECK YOUR EQUIPMENT

Look at your clubs. Are the faces worn? Heads cracked? Shafts bent? Most of these conditions can be repaired, but it might be time for a new set. And don't neglect the grips: If they're worn, the club can slip in your hands, leading to mis-hits. Replacing grips is cheap and easy.

. . . AND MORE

Practice, Practice, Practice

Good Golf Etiquette

Fun in the Fall

Buy Clubs That Fit

No Time to Warm Up?

Don't Waste the Winter

PRACTICE, PRACTICE, PRACTICE

Practice doesn't make perfect; only perfect practice makes perfect. To make the most of your practice sessions, follow these suggestions.

FOR ALL PRACTICE

Approach every session with a goal, be it working on your long game, getting used to grip change, or ironing out a fault. Have an objective and a plan to meet it.

Find a level spot that offers good lies, somewhere you can spread out without being interrupted. Loosen up gradually: Don't rush. Most important, always hit to a target, real or imaginary, no matter what part of the game you're working on.

LONG GAME

Know your distance with each club. Even if you have to walk off the yardage, don't swing simply to watch the ball in the air.

Lay two clubs on the ground, parallel to each other and aiming at your target, one across your toes, the other outside the ball. Regularly check your alignment against these clubs.

Hit enough balls to see patterns develop: Are you hitting left or right of the target? Which shot pattern and trajectory do you prefer? Are your distances fairly consistent?

Try changing your grip, alignment, and stance to see how shots are affected. Make notes of the results.

Practice putting with a striped range ball. When the stripe rolls straight, you're making good contact.

SHORT GAME

The keys to a good short game are club selection, a smooth, easy swing, and imagination. Practice can improve all three.

Practice chipping to a green, varying clubs, and hitting to different holes. Chip from good and bad lies. Vary the combinations of club, lie, and hole to see how the ball flies and rolls. (If possible, practice the short game with the ball you use in play; range balls don't give the same feel or performance as game balls.)

Practice pitch shots using different wedges. Invent games, trying to hit within a few feet of the same ball, or progressively hitting longer and shorter from a target. Hit over a bush or golf bag to simulate lofting over sand or water.

In the sand, change clubs and lies—uphill, downhill, buried, under the lip, and so on. Even if you don't master every situation, you'll learn how the ball performs.

PUTTING

Concentrate on a smooth, accelerating stroke and making contact on the sweetspot. Hit long and short putts, and try both left and right breaks. Also practice reading greens.

For good feedback, putt with a striped range ball. Watch the stripe: If it wobbles, you're not making solid contact. Keep practicing until the stripe rolls straight.

GOOD GOLF ETIQUETTE

One of golf's pleasures is that it is a game for gentlemen—and gentlewomen. To keep it that way, there exists a code of on-course conduct that will save the golfer both embarrassment and injury. Here are the basics of golf etiquette.

WHEN SOMEONE IS HITTING

Don't move, talk, or stand too close to the golfer preparing to swing. On the green be sure your shadow doesn't fall across the line of someone else's putt.

BE QUICK

A foursome should play 18 holes in four hours or less. To pick up the pace, think about your shot as you walk to it and be ready to hit when it's your turn. If you have to leave the cart or caddie and walk to your ball, take extra clubs. Don't dawdle before or after you've hit the shot. Don't give another golfer lessons during the round. Take your putter with you when walking to shot within 100 yards of the green. Don't spend more than five minutes looking for a lost ball, which leads to . . .

LET OTHERS PLAY THROUGH

If you are slow, looking for a lost ball, or are approached by a group smaller than yours (such as a single or a twosome), stand to the side and let them play through.

Think of the other players in your group and those who will follow. Repair your ball marks and at least one other.

Hold the flag to help on long putts.

REPAIR THE COURSE

Replace your divots. Fix your ball mark on the green and fix at least one other as well. Although the Rules of Golf prohibit tamping down spike-marks before you putt, you can clean them up after holing out. Don't drop the flagstick or extra clubs on the green; place them carefully. Don't lean on your putter while waiting on the green.

DON'T HIT WHEN OTHERS ARE IN RANGE

Assume you're going to hit a "career shot" and wait until players ahead are out of range. If a shot is heading toward other golfers, yell "Fore!"

IN THE SAND

Enter bunkers as close as possible to your ball, always at a level spot. Don't climb down steep banks if you don't have to. Bring the rake into the trap and smooth over footprints and other marks as you walk out. If there's no rake, use the clubhead.

ON THE GREEN

Be quiet when others are putting. Offer to tend the flag. Don't step on other players' lines. Line up your putt while others are putting. When the hole is through, walk off quickly. Write down scores after leaving the green.

In short, play safe, play smart, and do unto others.

FUN IN THE FALL

Autumn offers golfers many joys: crisp breezes, spectacular scenery, and less crowded courses. But playing in the fall presents problems as well, notably dealing with the leaves, pine needles, and other bits of nature that cover the ground.

If you find your ball in a bed of fallen leaves or pine needles, play it as you would from sand. For a long shot, set up as if in a fairway bunker: Open your stance slightly, center the ball between your feet, and angle your hands forward. Make a low takeaway and hit the ball before contacting the ground.

For a shorter shot, play it like an explosion: Open your stance and the blade, and hit an inch or so behind the ball. Keep your wrists firm so the clubface stays open through impact. Try a pitching wedge, which has a sharper leading edge than a sand club; it will cut easily through the leaves.

Be careful not to press the clubhead into the leaves before the shot. That could cause the ball to move, which is a one-shot penalty.

Another problem with leaves isn't hitting the ball, but finding it. Say you've seen your shot fly toward a pile of leaves but then can't locate it: Do you declare it lost—and hit again from the tee while adding a penalty stroke—or do you invoke the so-called "leaf rule," dropping a ball near the leaves and hitting without penalty?

The USGA notes that many clubs adopts the leaf rule as a local option, even though, strictly speaking, it is contrary to the Rules of Golf. If the leaf rule is in effect where you play, you should be familiar with Rule 25-1c, which says, "Unless there is reasonable evidence that a

Hover the club above the leaves so the ball doesn't move and cost you a penalty stroke.

ball which cannot be found is lost in the leaves, it must be treated as lost elsewhere" and the lost-ball rule applies.

Which means you should watch your shots—and your opponents'—closely. Allow a drop only if you're convinced the ball was heading for the leaves. Otherwise follow the rules, hit again, and take your medicine.

BUY CLUBS THAT FIT

If you're shopping for golf clubs, there are many questions to ask: Oversized heads? How much loft? Traditional irons or perimeter-weighted? Steel, graphite, or a more exotic shaft?

Answers to the above should be based on personal preference and how you play the game. But no matter what clubs you select, don't buy without having them fitted to you by a qualified pro or salesman. Here are the key clubfitting concerns. (You may need to special order to get the right fit; it's worth it!)

GRIP

If a grip is too big, wrist actions is inhibited, leading to a slice. Grips too small let the wrists roll over too easily, producing hooks. To find your right size, hold the grip in your left hand; your fingertips should just touch your palm. If your fingernails dig into your palm, the grip is too small; if there's more than an eighth-of-an-inch between fingers and palm, it's too big.

LENGTH

Clubs come in standard lengths that fit the vast majority of golfers; special lengths make sense only if you are unusually tall or short. Some players like longer clubs because they launch longer shots; however, they also are harder to control. Shorter clubs offer more accuracy, but at the expense of distance.

When the grip is right, your fingertips should just touch your palm.

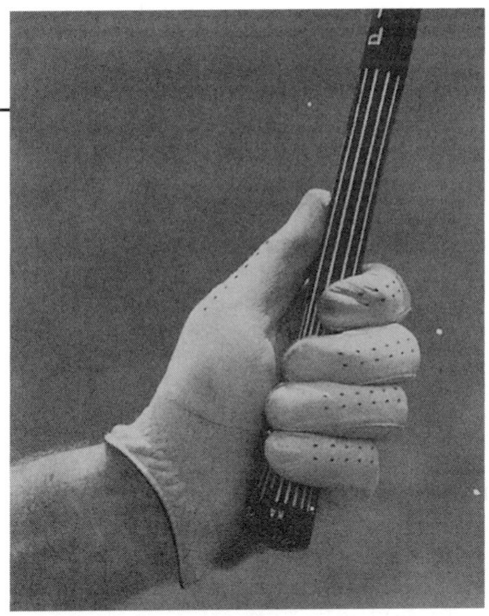

If they dig in, the grip is too small.

LIE ANGLE

This is the angle between the shaft and clubhead. Properly fit, the entire sole of the club will be on the ground at address. If the lie angle is too upright, you're forced to lower your hands, which raises the toe of the club off the ground and produces shots that fly left; a flat angle leads to slices.

Changing lie angle can help a tall or short player. The taller golfer should try a steeper lie angle, the shorter player a flatter angle.

SHAFT FLEX

There are no absolutes when choosing shaft flex, other than to try before you buy because the wrong flex causes wild shots. As a general rule, the stronger, faster-swinging golfer can handle a stiffer shaft. Most male amateurs will do fine with a regular flex. Ladies, seniors, and juniors should start with a softer flex.

Shafts of the same flex and material from different companies won't necessarily feel or perform the same way, which is why you should experiment with different combinations of shaft flex, shaft material, and clubhead. Watch the resulting shot patterns and be especially aware of the feel both during the swing and at impact.

NO TIME TO WARM UP?

Despite your best intentions, sometimes you arrive at the golf course without enough time for a full warm-up session. If that's the case, you have to expect some sloppy play on the opening holes. But there are ways to make the most of a rusty game over the first few holes.

First, don't attempt a swing without taking at least two minutes to stretch. Work the upper and lower body, especially the big muscles of the chest, back, and shoulders. Get the blood moving in your legs. Slowly swing a couple of clubs, trying to make a full follow-through.

When teeing off, put away your driver and take a 3-wood or 2-iron instead. Over the first few holes, give up a little distance for accuracy. And fight the natural urge to make a fast swing: Drag the club away from the ball as slowly as you can.

Since your woods and long irons probably won't be sharp at the start, you'll have to rely on your short game to keep competitive. If you have five minutes and a putting green, you can warm up your finesse game. You're going to need it.

Start by hitting a couple of chips with the 6-, 7-, and 8-irons. Don't aim them all at the same cup: Look for a variety of slopes, lengths, and if possible, breaks. Don't worry about the results; work on making solid contact.

With your pitching wedge, loft three or four soft shots at the green. Again, results aren't important; height and roll are. Swing easy so you feel the club.

If there's a practice bunker, hit a few shots from the sand. You'll probably find the sand early since your long game won't be sharp. A few swings in the bunker also will tell you about the condition of the sand.

Don't take even one practice swing without stretching the upper and lower body.

Stroke a few putts, starting with a couple from short range, then moving back 6 to 10 feet. Concentrate on making a good stroke and hitting the ball off the sweetspot of the putter.

Finally, roll two or three putts from about 20 feet. You can expect to face putts in this range before your game begins to click. When practicing long putts, look for break and speed of the green. Concentrate on good mechanics and making an aggressive stroke.

This quick practice can't guarantee that you'll play brilliantly on the early holes, but it should keep you in the match and on course for a fun round.

DON'T WASTE THE WINTER

Winter is approaching, which means many golfers will be putting their clubs away for a few months. Rather than letting your game go flat in the off-season, here are some practice tips and practical ways to keep your game sharp.

EXERCISE

A regimen of stretching exercises will help you make a bigger turn, whereas jogging will put spring in your legs for more lower-body action on the downswing. Both will mean longer shots.

SWING A WEIGHTED CLUB

Buy a heavyweight practice club or weighted "donut" that fits around the shaft of your driver, and swing it for 10 minutes a day to keep your muscles loose. The extra weight also encourages making a smooth, one-piece takeaway and an accelerating downswing.

INDOOR CHIPPING

Work on short-game feel by chipping off a rug into a chair. Don't worry about distance; try to keep the feeling of proper club-to-ball contact.

PRACTICE PUTTING

When putting on a carpet, think about the feel of a good stroke. Play some games: Put pressure on yourself by putting to a spot, and don't quit until you've "holed" a few. Hit long putts as well as short ones to get practice judging distance.

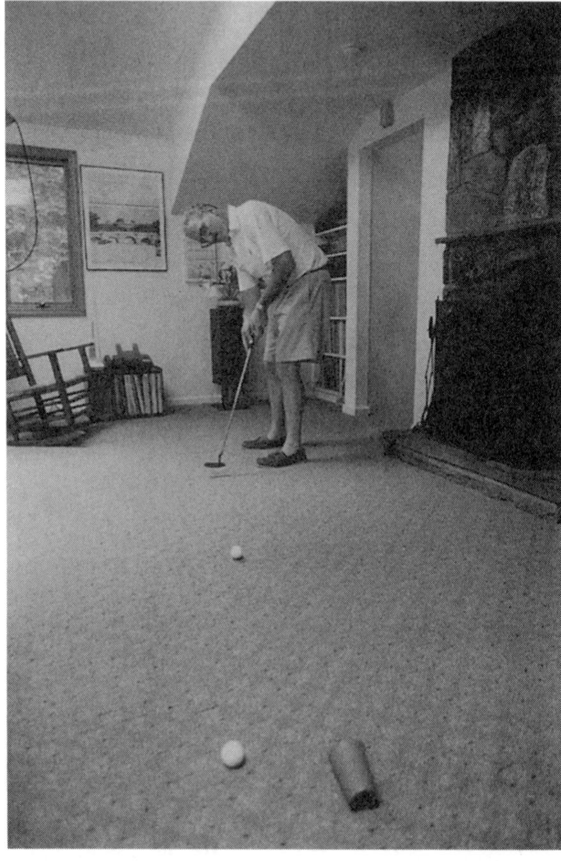

Putt on the carpet to keep your stroke grooved.

GRAB A GRIP

When the new season starts, many players report that their hands have forgotten how to take a grip. Retain your feel over the winter by cutting down an old club, keeping the grip end by your favorite easy chair, and taking hold for a few minutes every night.

CHART YOUR COURSE

On a clear fall or winter afternoon when no one is playing compile a personal yardage book by walking your regular course. Pace off distances from sprinkler heads, bunkers, trees, and other landmarks, especially your well-visited areas of the rough.

CHECK YOUR CLUBS

If you do put your clubs away for the winter, clean them first. Remove dirt and grass from the grooves, rub off any rust or dirt, and be sure the grips and the inside of the bag are dry; water leads to more rust and deterioration of rubber or leather grips. A quick toweling off will mean your clubs are ready to go when you are come spring.

INDEX